Matt Slater

CW01594288

LCP Spanish School Dictionary

Commissioning Editor
Teresa Adams

Editorial
Nicola Lusby • Anna Samuels • Kathryn Tate

Design
Simon Dainty • Antony Dickens • Sara Hemp

LCP
Hampton House
Longfield Road
Leamington Spa
Warwickshire
CV31 1XB
tel: 01926 886914 • **fax:** 01926 887136
e-mail: mail@LCP.co.uk • **website:** www.LCP.co.uk

First published 2004

ISBN 1 904178 46 4

A B C D E F G H I J K L M N O P Q R S T U V W X Y Z

LCP Spanish School Dictionary

The ***LCP* Spanish School Dictionary** is a dictionary for beginners of Spanish. It is an easy introduction to a bilingual dictionary to give you confidence in looking up words and then using them.

Unlike a standard dictionary, it is fully colour-coded for your ease of use. All headwords are listed alphabetically, with four main types of words in different colours.

- Any word printed in *green* is a verb (e.g. *comer*), or part of a verb (e.g. *tengo* from *tener*), or the reflexive part of a reflexive verb (e.g. the *se* in *se acuesta*). Before you can fully understand the meaning of a verb, you need to look at its tense and its endings. For example, *comer* is listed as 'to eat', but in the context in which you find it, it might be *comió* ('he ate'). Irregular forms are also listed alphabetically, e.g. *fui* is listed as meaning 'I was/went'.

  Equally, if you look up the English words 'to eat', you will find *comer*. But before you can use it, you will probably need to change the ending. The appendix at the back of the dictionary will help you find the correct ending to use.

- Any word in *red* is a feminine noun (e.g. *la hija* = 'girl').
- Any word in *blue* is a masculine noun (e.g. *el hombre* = 'man').

- Any *purple* word is an adjective (e.g. *bonito*). These words describe nouns and have to change their endings accordingly. The 'o' changes to an 'a' if the noun is feminine (e.g. *una casa pequeña*) and an 's' is added if the noun is plural (e.g. *dos casas pequeñas*). If the feminine form is not just an 'a' instead of an 'o' at the end of the word, then the full form is given for easy reference (e.g. *alemán/alemana*).

Some words have more than one meaning, and you need to decide which is the more suitable meaning from the passage in which the word occurs.

The two headwords at the top of each page show the first and last word dealt with.

The alphabet is printed on each page showing the featured letter in yellow, so that you can find the word you are looking for more easily.

There is a colour code reminder at the bottom of each page.

= masculine noun   = feminine noun   = verb   = adjective

The dictionary also includes at the back a useful appendix of such areas as numbers, days of the week, months, times and seasons.

español – inglés

Aa

	a	to
	abajo	downstairs, below
el	abanico	fan
el	abecedario	alphabet
	abierto	open
el	abogado	lawyer
el	abrazo	hug
un	abrazo	love from (in a letter)
	abrazos	lots of love
	abrid	open (*vosotros* command)
el	abrigo	overcoat, coat
	abril	April
	abrir	to open
la	abuela	grandmother
el	abuelo	grandfather
los	abuelos	grandparents
	aburrido	boring, bored
	acabar	to finish
	acabar de	to have just
el	accesorio	accessory
la	acción	action
el	aceite (de oliva)	(olive) oil
la	aceituna	olive
	aceptar	to accept
la	acera	pavement
el	acero	steel
	a (cinco) minutos andando	a (five-) minute walk away
	a (cinco) minutos en coche	(five) minutes by car
	acogedor	cosy
	acordarse de	to remember
	acostarse	to go to bed
la	actividad	activity
	activo	active
el	actor	actor
la	actriz	actress
	actualmente	now, currently
	acuático	water
el	acueducto	aqueduct
de	acuerdo	OK
se	acuesta (a)	he/she goes to bed (at)
te	acuestas (a)	you go to bed (at)

A B C D E F G H I J K L M N O P Q R S T U V W X Y Z

A B C D E F G H I J K L M N O P Q R S T U V W X Y Z

me	**acuesto (a)**	I go to bed (at)
	adecuado	appropriate
	adelante	forward
	además	besides, in addition
	a (diez) kilómetros	(ten) kilometres away
	adiós	goodbye
	adivinar	to guess
el	**adjetivo**	adjective
	adjuntar	to enclose, to attach
	¿adónde?	where (to)?
	¿adónde vas?	where are you going? (*tú*, informal)
	adornar	to decorate
	adoro	I love, I adore
	adosado	semi-detached
el	**aeropuerto**	airport
	afeitarse	to shave
	aficionado	keen, enthusiastic
	Africa	Africa
	africano	African
(en) las	**afueras**	(on) the outskirts, suburbs
la	**agenda**	diary
	agosto	August
	agotado	exhausted
	agradable	pleasant
el	**agricultor**	farmer (male)
la	**agricultora**	farmer (female)
el	**agua**	water
el	**agua mineral**	mineral water
el	**agujero**	hole
	ahí	over there
	ahora	now
	ahorrar	to save
el	**aire libre**	open air, fresh air, outdoor(s)
el	**ajedrez**	chess
el	**ajo**	garlic
	ajustado	tight, tight-fitting
	al	to the
	a la	to the
	a las dos	at two o'clock
	a la una	at one o'clock
el	**albergue juvenil**	youth hostel
el	**alcalde**	mayor
la	**alcaldesa**	mayoress
el	**alcázar**	fortress, palace

■ = masculine noun ■ = feminine noun ■ = verb ■ = adjective

la	aldea	village, hamlet
	alegre	happy
la	alegría	happiness
	alemán/alemana	German
el	alemán	German (language)
el	alemán	German person (male)
la	alemana	German person (female)
la	Alemania	Germany
el	alfabeto	alphabet
la	alfombra	rug, carpet
	algo	something
el	algodón	cotton
	alguien	somebody
	algún/algunos/algunas	some
en	alguna parte	somewhere
los	alimentos	foods
	allá	over there
	al lado de	beside
	allí	there
el	almacén	department store
las (grandes)	almacenes	department store
el	alojamiento	lodgings
nos	alojamos	we stay(ed)
	alojarse	to stay, to lodge
me	alojé	I stayed
el	alpinismo	climbing, mountaineering
	alquilamos	we hire(d)
	alquilar	to hire
	alrededor (de)	around
	alto	high, tall
la	altura	height
la	alumna	pupil (female)
el	alumno	pupil (male)
	amable	kind
la	ama de casa	housewife
	amarillo	yellow
el	ambiente	atmosphere, environment
	ambos	both
la	amenaza	threat
	a menudo	often
la	América del Sur	South America
	americano	American
la	amiga	friend (female)
la	amiga por correspondencia	penfriend (female)

A B C D E F G H I J K L M N O P Q R S T U V W X Y Z

■ = masculine noun ■ = feminine noun ■ = verb ■ = adjective

el **amigo**	friend (male)
el **amigo por correspondencia**	penfriend (male)
la **amistad**	friendship
añadir	to add
el **análisis**	analysis
ancho	wide
la **anchoa**	anchovy
la **anchura**	width
¡ándale!	go on!
andando	walking
andar	to walk
andar en monopatín	to go skateboarding
el **anillo**	ring
animado	lively
el **animal**	animal, pet
el **año**	year
el **Año Nuevo**	New Year
anteayer	the day before yesterday
anteriormente	previously
antes (de)	before
antiguo	old
antillano	West Indian
antipático	unkind, unpleasant
antiséptico	antiseptic
el **anuncio**	advert
apagar	to switch off
el **aparcamiento**	car park
aparcar	to park
el **apartamento**	apartment
a partir de	from
el **apellido**	surname
aprender	to learn
apretar	to press
apropiado	correct
apto	suitable
aquél, aquélla	that, that one
aquellos	those
aquí	here
la **araña**	spider
el **árbol**	tree
la **arena**	sand
Argentina	Argentina
argentino	Argentinian
el **argumento**	plot

el **armario**	wardrobe, cupboard
el **arquitecto**	architect
arreglar	to tidy, to tidy up, to sort out
arreglo (mi dormitorio)	I tidy (my bedroom)
arriba	upstairs, above
arriesgar	to risk
arroba	@
el **arroz**	rice
la **artesanía**	craftwork
el **artículo**	article, object
artístico	artistic
el **ascensor**	lift
el **aseo**	toilet
asesinar	to murder
así	so, thus
la **asignación**	pocket money
la **asignatura**	subject, school subject
asistir	to attend
la **aspiradora**	vacuum cleaner, hoover
pasar la **aspiradora**	to vacuum
la **aspirina**	aspirin
asustado	frightened
el **atasco**	traffic jam
la **atención**	attention
el **ático**	attic
a tiempo	on time
atigrado	tabby (cat)
el **atleta**	athlete (male)
la **atleta**	athlete (female)
el **atletismo**	athletics
la **atracción**	attraction
(de) **atrás**	behind
el **atún**	tuna
el **aula**	classroom
aún	still, yet
aunque	although
aun (si)	even (if)
los **auriculares**	head/earphones
Australia	Australia
australiano	Australian
Austria	Austria
austríaco	Austrian
el **autobús**	bus
en **autobús**	by bus
el **autocar**	coach

■ = masculine noun ■ = feminine noun ■ = verb ■ = adjective

la	**autopista**	motorway
	a veces	sometimes
la	**avenida**	avenue
la	**aventura**	adventure
el	**avión**	aeroplane, plane
	avisar	to warn
el	**aviso**	warning
	ayer	yesterday
la	**ayuda**	help
	ayudar	to help
	¿ayudas (en casa)?	do you help (at home)? (*tú*, informal)
el	**ayuntamiento**	town hall
la	**azafata**	air stewardess
el	**azafato**	air steward
el	**azafrán**	saffron
la	**azotea**	flat roof
el	**azúcar**	sugar
	azul	blue

Bb

el bacalao	cod
el bachillerato	sixth-form course
el bádminton	badminton
bailar	to dance
bailé	I danced
el baile	dance
baja	go down (*tú* command)
bajar	to go down, to lower
bajar de	to get off (bus)
bajo	below, under
bajo	short, low
el bajo	bass (musical instrument)
salir en balandro	to go sailing
el balcón	balcony
el baloncesto	basketball
el balonmano	handball
el bañador	swimming costume/trunks
bañarse	to have a bath, to bathe
el banco	bank
la bandera	flag
el baño	bathroom
el bar	bar
barato	cheap, inexpensive
la barba	beard
la barbacoa	barbecue
la barbilla	chin
el barco (de vela)	(sailing) boat
la barra de pan	loaf of bread
barrer	to sweep
el barrio	the neighbourhood
barro	I sweep
bastante	quite, enough
la basura	rubbish
el basurero	refuse collector
la batalla	battle
la batería	drums
el batido	milkshake
bebe	drink (*tú* command)
el bebé	baby
beber	to drink
bebes	you drink (*tú*, informal)
la bebida	drink

A B C D E F G H I J K L M N O P Q R S T U V W X Y Z

el **béisbol**	baseball
el **belén**	nativity scene
bello	beautiful
besar	to kiss
el **beso**	kiss
la **biblioteca**	library
en **bici**	by bike
la **bicicleta**	bicycle
la **bicicleta de montaña**	mountain bike
bien	fine, well
bienvenido	welcome!
bienvenido	welcome
el **biftec**	steak
el **bigote**	moustache
bilingüe	bilingual
el **billete**	note (money), ticket (transport)
la **bisabuela**	great-grandmother
el **bisabuelo**	great-grandfather
el **bistec**	steak
blanco	white
el **bloque**	block of flats
la **blusa**	blouse
la **boca**	mouth
el **bocadillo**	sandwich (with crusty bread)
la **boda**	wedding
la **bodega**	wine cellar
la **boina**	beret
la **bolera**	bowling alley
el **boletín**	school report
el **bolígrafo**	ballpoint pen
la **bolsa**	bag
el **bolsillo**	pocket
el **bolso**	handbag
lo **pasé bomba**	I had a great time
el **bombero**	firefighter
los **bombones**	sweets, chocolates
bonito	good-looking, pretty
el **bonito**	bonito fish
el **borde**	edge
bordear	to border
el **borrador**	rough copy
el **bosque**	woods, forest
la **bota**	boot
la **botella**	bottle
el **botón**	button

■ = masculine noun ■ = feminine noun ■ = verb ■ = adjective

A B C D E F G H I J K L M N O P Q R S T U V W X Y Z

la	braga	knickers
	Brasil	Brazil
	brasileño	Brazilian
el	brazo	arm
el	bricolaje	DIY
	brillar	to shine
la	broma	joke
el	bronceado	suntan
el	bronceador	suntan lotion
la	bruja	witch
la	brújula	compass
	bucear	to dive
	buena idea	good idea
	buenas noches	goodnight
	buena suerte	good luck
	buenas tardes	good afternoon/evening
	buenísimo	very good
	bueno	good
	buenos días	good morning
la	bufanda	scarf
	busca	search, look (*tú* command)
el	buscador	search engine
	buscar	to look for
	buscar y reemplazar	to find and replace
la	butaca	armchair
el	buzeo	diving
el	buzón	post box

A B **C** D E F G H I J K L M N O P Q R S T U V W X Y Z

Cc

la	cabalgata	parade
el	caballero	gentleman
el	caballo	horse
la	cabeza	head
los	cacahuetes	peanuts
	cada	every, each
la	cadena	hi-fi/sound system, TV channel
	caer	to fall
el	café	coffee
el	café con leche	white coffee
el	café de Internet	Internet café
la	cafetería	cafeteria
la	caja	box
los	calamares	squid
el	calcetín	sock
la	calculadora	calculator
el	calendario	calendar
la	calidad	quality
	caliente	hot, warm
	callado	silent
la	calle	street
la	calle principal	main street
el	calor	heat
hace	calor	it's hot
	calzar	to take (shoe size)
los	calzoncillos	underpants
la	cama	bed
la	camarera	waitress
el	camarero	waiter
	cambiar	to change, to exchange
el	cambio	change, exchange
el	camello	camel
el	camino	path
el	camión	lorry
la	camioneta	van
la	camisa	shirt
la	camiseta	T-shirt, vest
el	campamento	campsite, summer camp
la	campana	bell
el	camping	campsite, camping
el	campo	countryside, field
la	caña de pesca	fishing rod

■ = masculine noun ■ = feminine noun ■ = verb ■ = adjectiv

el canal	TV channel
cancelar	to delete
la cancha	court
la canción	song
trabajar de canguro	to do babysitting
cansado	tired
el cantante	singer (male)
la cantante	singer (female)
cantar	to sing
la cantidad	quantity
la cantimplora	flask
la capa	layer
capaz (de)	capable (of)
la capital	capital
la capucha	hood
la cara	face
el caracol	snail
el carácter	character
¡caramba!	goodness!
los caramelos	sweets
la cárcel	prison
el Caribe	the Caribbean
cariñoso	loving, caring
la carne	meat
el carnet de conducir	driving licence
la carnicera	butcher (female)
la carnicería	butcher's
el carnicero	butcher (male)
caro	expensive
la carpeta	file
el carpintero	carpenter
la carrera	race
la carta	letter, menu
las cartas	playing cards
cartear	to correspond, to write to
la cartera	school bag, wallet, postwoman
el cartero	postman
el cartón	cardboard
en casa	at home
la casa	house
la casa de mis sueños	my dream house
casado	married
casar	to marry
el casco	helmet
el caserío	Basque farmhouse

■ = masculine noun ■ = feminine noun ■ = verb ■ = adjective

A B C D E F G H I J K L M N O P Q R S T U V W X Y Z

el **casete**	cassette player
la **casete**	(audio) cassette
casi	almost, nearly
castaño	brown
las **castañuelas**	castanets
castellano	Spanish, Castilian
castigar	to punish
Castilla	Castille
el **castillo**	castle
el **catalán**	Catalan
el **catálogo**	catalogue
la **Cataluña**	Catalonia
tener catarro	to have a cold
la **catedral**	cathedral
la **categoría**	category
católico	Catholic
catorce	fourteen
(a) causa de	because of
la **caza**	hunting
cazar	to hunt
el **CD**	CD
la **cebolla**	onion
la **cebra**	zebra
la **ceja**	eyebrow
celebramos	we celebrate
celebrar	to celebrate
celoso	jealous
la **cena**	supper, dinner
cenar	to have supper, dinner
cenas	you have supper, dinner (*tú*, informal)
ceno	I have supper, dinner
el **céntimo**	cent
el **centro**	(town) centre
el **centro comercial**	shopping centre
el **cepillo de dientes**	toothbrush
el **cepillo para el pelo**	hairbrush
la **cerámica**	pottery
cerca (de)	near (to)
el **cerdo**	pig, pork
los **cereales**	cereal
la **cereza**	cherry
la **cerilla**	match
cero	zero
cerrar	to close

■ = masculine noun ■ = feminine noun ■ = verb ■ = adjectiv

la	cerveza	beer
la	cesta	basket
el	chalet	house, chalet
el	champiñón	mushroom
el	champú	shampoo
las	chanclas	flip-flops
el	chándal	tracksuit
la	chaqueta	jacket
la	charcutería	delicatessen
	charlar	to chat
el	chaval	lad
la	chavala	lass
la	chica	girl
el	chicle	chewing gum
el	chico	boy
los	chicos	boys and girls
	Chile	Chile
	chileno	Chilean
la	chimenea	fireplace
	chino	Chinese
el	chocolate	chocolate
el	chorizo	spicy sausage
el	chubasco	downpour, shower
la	chuleta	(pork) chop
los	churros	fritters
el	ciclismo	cycling
el	ciclista	cyclist (male)
la	ciclista	cyclist (female)
	ciego	blind
el	cielo	sky
la	ciencia	science
la	ciencia-ficción	science fiction
las	ciencias	(combined) science
la	científica	scientist (female)
el	científico	scientist (male)
	cien(to)	one hundred
	cierto	certain
los	cigarillos	cigarettes
	cinco	five
	cincuenta	fifty
el	cine	cinema
la	cinta	tape
la	cintura	waist
el	cinturón	belt
el	círculo	circle

A B **C** D E F G H I J K L M N O P Q R S T U V W X Y Z

= masculine noun = feminine noun = verb = adjective

A B **C** D E F G H I J K L M N O P Q R S T U V W X Y Z

la	cita	appointment, date
la	ciudad	city, town
	claro	light, clear
la	clase	lesson, classroom
	clásico	classic
la	clave	key
el	clima	climate
el	club	club
el	cobayo	guinea pig
el	coche	car
en	coche	by car
el	cochinillo asado	roast suckling pig
el	cocido	stew
la	cocina	kitchen, cooker, cooking
	cocinar	to cook
la	cocinera	chef, cook (female)
el	cocinero	chef, cook (male)
el	código	code
el	codo	elbow
	coger	to catch, to grab
el	cojín	cushion
la	cola	queue, tail, glue
el	colchón	mattress
la	colección	collection
	coleccionar	to collect
el	colega	colleague (male)
la	colega	colleague (female)
el	colegio	school
la	colina	hill
	colocar	to place, to put
	colocarse	to be placed
	Colombia	Colombia
la	colonia	cologne
el	color	colour
la	columna vetebral	spine
el	combate	fight
	come	eat (*tú* command)
el	comedor	dining room, canteen
	comentar	to comment on
	comenzar	to begin, to start
	comer	to eat
el	comercio	business, commerce
	comes	you have lunch, you eat (*tú*, informal)
los	comestibles	food
	cómico	funny

■ = masculine noun ■ = feminine noun ■ = verb ■ = adjective

la **comida**	lunch/dinner, food, meal
la **comisaría**	police station
como	I eat/have lunch
como	as, like, how
¿cómo?	how?, what?
cómodo	comfortable
¿cómo eres?	what are you like? (*tú*, informal)
¿cómo es?	what's it like?
¿cómo estás?	how are you? (*tú*, informal)
¿cómo está usted?	how are you? (*usted*, formal)
¿cómo llegas al instituto?	how do you come/get to school?
¿cómo se dice ... en español?	how do you say ... in Spanish?
¿cómo se escribe tu nombre?	how do you spell your name?
¿cómo te llamas?	what's your name? (*tú*, informal)
la **compañera**	partner, colleague, classmate (female)
el **compañero**	partner, colleague, classmate (male)
compartir	to share
competir	to compete
complétalo	fill it in (*tú* command)
completar	to complete, to fill in
comprar	to buy
ir de **compras**	to go shopping
comprender	to understand
no **comprendo**	I don't understand
comprobar	to check
comprueba	check (*tú* command)
con	with
el **concurso**	competition
conducir	to drive
el **conductor**	driver (male)
la **conductora**	driver (female)
el **conejillo de Indias**	guinea pig
el **conejo**	rabbit
confirmar	to confirm
el **congelador**	freezer
congelar	to freeze
conmigo	with me
conocer	to know, to get to know
(muy) **conocido**	(well) known
conseguir	to win, to get
los **consejos**	advice
la **contaminación**	pollution

A B **C** D E F G H I J K L M N O P Q R S T U V W X Y Z

	contaminar	to pollute
	contar	to count
	contento	happy
	contesta	answer (*tú* command)
	contestar	to answer, to reply
	contiene	it contains
	contigo	with you
	contra	against
	contrarreloj	against the clock
la	**contraseña**	password
la	**conversación**	conversation
	convertirse (en)	to change (into)
la	**copa**	glass (for drinking)
	copia	copy (*tú* command)
	copiar	to copy
el	**coprotagonista**	co-star (male)
la	**coprotagonista**	co-star (female)
el	**corazón**	heart
la	**corbata**	tie
el	**cordero**	lamb
	correcto	correct, right
	corregir	to correct
el	**correo**	post
el	**correo electrónico**	e-mail
el	**Correos**	main post office
	correr	to run
la	**correspondencia**	correspondence
la	**corrida**	bullfight
	corriente	ordinary
	cortar	to cut (down)
	cortés/cortesa	polite
las	**cortinas**	curtains
	corto	short
la	**cosa**	thing
la	**costa**	coast
	costar	to cost
	Costa Rica	Costa Rica
	costarricense	Costa Rican
el	**costumbre**	custom, habit
	crecer	to grow
	creer	to believe
la	**crema**	cream
	creo	I think
el	**críquet**	cricket
el	**cristal**	glass
la	**cristiana**	Christian (female)

■ = masculine noun ■ = feminine noun ■ = verb ■ = adjective

el	cristianismo	Christianity
el	cristiano	Christian (male)
	cruel	cruel
	cruza	cross (*tú* command)
	cruzar	to cross
el	cuaderno	exercise book
el	cuadrado	square
el	cuadro	grid, chart, picture
	¿cuál?	what?, which?
la	cualidad	quality
	cuando	when
	¿cuándo?	when?
	¿cuándo es tu cumpleaños?	when is your birthday?
¿de	cuántas plantas es?	how many floors has it got?
	¿cuánto/a?	how much?
	¿cuánto hay…?	how far is it…?
	¿cuántos/cuántas?	how many?
	¿cuántos años tienes?	how old are you? (*tú*, informal)
	¿cuánto tiempo…?	how long…?
	cuarenta	forty
	cuarto	fourth
el	cuarto	room, quarter, (the) fourth
el	cuarto de baño	bathroom
	cuatro	four
	cubano	Cuban
	cubrir	to cover
la	cuchara	spoon
el	cuchillo	knife
el	cuello	neck
la	cuenta	bill, account
darse	cuenta de	to realise
el	cuero	leather
el	cuerpo	body
	cuesta(n)	it/they cost(s)
la	cueva	cave
	¡cuidado!	be careful!
	cuidar	to take care of
la	culebra	snake
el	culebrón	soap opera
	cultivar	to grow, to cultivate
el	cumpleaños	birthday
	cumplir (años)	to have one's birthday
la	cuna	crib
el	curso	course, year

■ = masculine noun ■ = feminine noun ■ = verb ■ = adjective

A B C D E F G H I J K L M N O P Q R S T U V W X Y Z

Dd

el	dado	dice
	dando	giving
	dar	to give
	darse cuenta (de)	to realise
los	datos	data, details
	de	about, from, of
	de acuerdo	agreed, OK
	debajo (de)	below, underneath
	debe	he/she/it should
	deber	to owe, to have to, must
los	deberes	homework
	débil	weak
	decepcionado	disappointed
	decidir	to decide
	décimo	tenth
	decir	to say, to tell
el	dedo	finger
el	dedo gordo	big toe
el	dedo pulgar	thumb
	deficiente	inadequate
la	deforestación	deforestation
	déjame	could you lend me ...
	dejar	to leave
	del	of, from the
	delante (de)	in front (of)
	deletrear	to spell out
	delgado	slim, thin
	delicioso	delicious
lo	demás	the other, the rest
	demasiado	too much, too many
	deme	give me (*usted* command)
el	dentista	dentist (male)
la	dentista	dentist (female)
	dentro (de)	inside, within
la	dependienta	shop assistant (female)
el	dependiente	shop assistant (male)
el	deporte	sport
el	deportista	sportsman
la	deportista	sportswoman
	deportivo	sporty
	deprimido	depressed
la	derecha	right (direction)

= masculine noun = feminine noun = verb = adjectiv

a la **derecha (de)**	to the right (of)
el **desastre**	disaster
desayunar	to have breakfast
desayunas	you have breakfast (*tú*, informal)
el **desayuno**	breakfast
desayuno (...)	I have breakfast, for breakfast I have ...
descansar	to rest
el **descanso**	rest
descargar	to download
desconocido	unknown
describiendo	describing
describir	to describe
la **descripción**	description
desde	from, since
desde luego	of course
desear	to want, to wish
el **desfile**	street procession
por **desgracia**	unfortunately
el **desodorante**	deodorant
desordenado	untidy
el **despacho**	office
despacio	slow
despedirse (de)	to say goodbye (to)
el **despertador**	alarm clock
despertar(se)	to wake up
te **despiertas**	you wake up
(no) me **despierto**	I (don't) wake up
después	afterwards, then
después de (cenar)	after (dinner)
la **destrucción**	destruction
destruir	to destroy
el **desván**	attic, loft
la **desventaja**	disadvantage
el **detalle**	detail
detestar	to detest
detrás (de)	behind
devolver	to refund
di	say (*tú* command)
el **día**	day
muy al **día**	very trendy
día de los Muertos	Day of the Dead
el **diálogo**	dialogue
diario	daily

A B C D E F G H I J K L M N O P Q R S T U V W X Y Z

■ = masculine noun ■ = feminine noun ■ = verb ■ = adjective

A B C D E F G H I J K L M N O P Q R S T U V W X Y Z

el diario	diary
la diarrea	diarrhoea
todos los días	every day
dibujar	to draw, to sketch
el dibujo	art (subject), drawing, picture
los dibujos animados	cartoons
el diccionario	dictionary
diciembre	December
diecinueve	nineteen
dieciocho	eighteen
dieciséis	sixteen
diecisiete	seventeen
el diente	tooth
la dieta	diet
diez	ten
la diferencia	difference
diferente	different
difícil	difficult
¿diga?/¿dígame?	hello? (on phone)
el dinero	money
el dios	god
la dirección	address
la dirección de la red	website address
las direcciones	directions, addresses
el director	headteacher (male)
la directora	headteacher (female)
el disco	disc
el disco compacto	CD, compact disc
la discoteca	nightclub
discutir	to discuss
diseña	design (*tú* command)
diseñado	designed
el disfraz	disguise, fancy dress
el disquete	floppy disk
la distancia	distance
la diversión	fun
divertido	fun, amusing
divertirse	to enjoy oneself, to have fun
se divierte	he/she has fun
me divierto	I have fun
dobla	turn (*tú* command)
doler	to hurt
el dolor (de cabeza)	hurt, pain (headache)
(el) domingo	(on) Sunday
la República Dominicana	the Dominican Republic

■ = masculine noun ■ = feminine noun ■ = verb ■ = adjective

dominicano	Dominican
Don	Mr (for older people)
Doña	Mrs/Ms (for older people)
donde	where
¿dónde?	where?
¿de dónde eres?	where are you from? (*tú*, informal)
¿dónde está?	where is it?
¿dónde nos encontramos?	where shall we meet?
¿dónde quedamos?	where shall we meet?
¿dónde vive ...?	where does ... live?
¿dónde vives?	where do you live? (*tú*, informal)
dorado	golden
dormir	to sleep
el dormitorio	bedroom
dos	two
dos veces	twice
la droga	drug
la ducha	shower
ducharse	to shower
te duchas	you have a shower (*tú*, informal)
me ducho	I have a shower
me duele el brazo	my arm hurts
la dueña	owner (female)
el dueño	owner (male)
dulce	sweet, kind
durante	in, during, for (time)
durante la semana	on weekdays
durar	to last
duro	hard
el DVD	DVD
el lector de DVD	DVD player

A B C D E F G H I J K L M N O P Q R S T U V W X Y Z

A B C D **E** F G H I J K L M N O P Q R S T U V W X Y Z

Ee

e	and (before *i* and *hi*)
echar	to throw
echar al buzón/correo	to post
Ecuador	Ecuador
ecuatoriano	Ecuadorean
la edad	age
edificar	to build
el edificio	building
la educación física	physical education, PE
los EE.UU.	USA
egoísta	selfish
el ejemplo	example
por ejemplo	for example
el ejercicio	exercise
él	he, him, it
el	the
la electricidad	electricity
los electrodomésticos	domestic appliances
electrónico	electronic
el elefante	elephant
elegante	elegant
elige	choose (*tú* command)
ella	she, it
ellos/ellas	they
El Salvador	El Salvador
sin embargo	however
la emoción	emotion
emocionante	exciting, moving
el emoticón	'smiley'
emparejar	to match up
empezar	to begin, to start
empieza	it begins
empiezan	they begin
la empleada	employee (female)
el empleado	employee (male)
emplear	to use
el empleo	employment, job
empujar	to push
en	in, on, at
(me) encanta	I love it, I like it a lot
encantado	pleased to meet you
encantar (a)	to delight

■ = masculine noun ■ = feminine noun ■ = verb ■ = adjectiv

	encargar	to order (meal)
	empujar	to push
	encender	to switch on
	encima (de)	on (top) (of)
nos	**encontramos**	we meet/met
	encontrar	to find
	encontrarse (con)	to meet
se	**encuentran**	they meet
la	**encuesta**	survey
la	**energía**	energy
	enero	January
	enfadado	angry, cross
	enfadarse	to get cross
la	**enfermedad**	illness
la	**enfermera**	nurse (female)
el	**enfermero**	nurse (male)
	enfermo	ill
	enfrente (de)	opposite, in front (of)
	¡enhorabuena!	congratulations!
	enorme	enormous, huge
la	**ensalada**	salad
	enseguida	straight away
	enseñar	to teach
	entender	to understand
	entero	whole
	entonces	then
desde	**entonces**	since then
en la	**entrada**	at the entrance
la	**entrada**	entrance, hallway, entrance ticket
	entrar	to enter, to go in
	entrar al sistema	to log on
	entre	amongst, between
el	**entremés**	starter
	entrenar	to train
el	**entrenedor**	sports coach
la	**entrevista**	interview
	envía	send (*tú* command)
	envíanos	send us
	enviar	to send
la	**época**	period of time, season, age
el	**equipo**	equipment, team
el	**equipo de fútbol**	football team
el	**equipo de música**	sound system
la	**equitación**	horse riding
	equivocarse	to make a mistake

	era	he/she/it was, you were (*usted*, formal)
	eres	you are (*tú*, informal)
	¿eres ...?	are you ...?
el	**error**	mistake
	es	he/she/it is, you are (*usted*, formal)
la	**escalada**	climbing
la	**escalera**	stairs
	escocés/escocesa	Scottish
	Escocia	Scotland
me	**escribas**	write to me
	escríbeme pronto	write to me soon
	escribid	write (*vosotros* command)
	escribir	to write
el	**escritorio**	writing desk
	escuchad	listen (*vosotros* command)
	escuchar	to listen
	escuchar música	to listen to music
la	**escuela (primaria)**	(primary) school
el	**escúter**	scooter
	¡es divertido!	it's fun!
	ese/esa	that
	ése/ésa	that one
	esforzarse	to make an effort
el	**esfuerzo**	effort
	es la una	it's one o'clock
	ESO (Educación Secundaria Obligatoria)	secondary school education
	esos/esas	those
	ésos/ésas	those ones
	espacial	space
los	**espaguetis**	spaghetti
la	**espalda**	back
	España	Spain
el	**español**	Spanish (language)
	español(a)	Spanish
la	**especia**	species
	especial	special
	especialmente	especially
	espectacular	spectacular
el	**espectáculo**	show, performance
el	**espejo**	mirror
la	**espeleología**	potholing
	esperar	to hope, to wait
	espero	I hope

■ = masculine noun ■ = feminine noun ■ = verb ■ = adjective

	espeso	thick
el	esqueleto	skeleton
el	esquí	skiing
	esquiar	to ski
	esta	this
	está	he/she/it is
ya	está	that's it
	está bien	it's alright, OK
la	estación	station
la	estación de autobuses	bus station
la	estación de esquí	ski resort
la	estación (del año)	season (of the year)
la	estación de servicio	petrol station
la	estación de trenes/de RENFE	train station
la	estación espacial	space station
el	estadio	stadium
los	Estados Unidos	the United States
	estadounidense	American
	está en ...	it's in ...
	esta mañana	this morning
	estampado	printed, patterned
el	estanco	tobacconist's
	esta noche	tonight
la	estantería	shelf, bookshelf
	estar	to be (location, state)
	estar resfriado/constipado	to have a cold
	esta tarde	this afternoon/evening
el	este	east
	este/esta	this
	éste/ésta/esto	this one
el	estereo	stereo
el	estereotipo	stereotype
el	estilo	style
el	estilo de vida	way of life
	estimado	dear (in a letter)
el	estómago	stomach
	estos/estas	these
	éstos/éstas	these ones
	estoy	I am
	estrecho	tight, narrow
la	estrella	star
	estresado	stressed
el	estuche	pencil case
el	estudiante	student (male)
la	estudiante	student (female)

A B C D E F G H I J K L M N O P Q R S T U V W X Y Z

= masculine noun = feminine noun = verb = adjective

A B C D E F G H I J K L M N O P Q R S T U V W X Y Z

estudiar	to study
estupendo	great, fantastic
estúpido	stupid
la etiqueta	label, sticker
la étnica	ethnically aware person (female)
el étnico	ethnically aware person (male)
el euro	euro
Europa	Europe
europeo	European
la evaluación	assessment
el examen	exam
excelente	excellent
la excursión	excursion, trip
el éxito	success
tener éxito	to be successful, to succeed
la experiencia	experience
el experimento	experiment
la explicación	explanation
explicar	to explain
explorar	to explore
la explosión	explosion
la exposición	presentation
extender	to stretch
el extranjero	abroad, overseas
extraño	strange
el extraterrestre	extraterrestrial
la extrovertida	extrovert (female)
el extrovertido	extrovert (male)

■ = masculine noun ■ = feminine noun ■ = verb ■ = adjecti

f

la	fábrica	factory
	fácil	easy
	fácilmente	easily
la	falda	skirt
	falso	false
	faltar	to miss, to be missing
la	familia	family
	famoso	famous
	fantástico	fantastic
la	farmacéutica	chemist (female)
el	farmacéutico	chemist (male)
la	farmacia	chemist shop
	fascinar	to fascinate
el	fast-food	fast-food restaurant
	fatal	terrible, awful, rotten
por	favor	please
	favorito	favourite
	febrero	February
la	fecha	date
la	felicidad	happiness
	feliz	happy
	¡feliz cumpleaños!	happy birthday!
	femenino	feminine
	fenomenal	great, brilliant, fantastic
	feo	ugly
la	feria	festival, funfair
el	ferrocarril	railway
la	ficha	form, card
el	fichero	form, file (computer)
la	fiebre	fever, temperature
tengo	fiebre	I have a fever, temperature
la	fiesta	festival, party
la	fila	row, line
el	filete	steak
el	fin	end (film)
el	final	end (event)
al	final (de)	at the end (of)
	finalmente	finally
la	finca	farm
el	fin de semana	(at) the weekend
los	fines de semana	(at) weekends
la	física	physics

A B C D E **F** G H I J K L M N O P Q R S T U V W X Y Z

el **flamenco**	flamenco (music, dance)
el **flan**	crème caramel
la **flauta**	flute
la **flor**	flower
el **florero**	vase
la **floristería**	flower shop
el **folleto**	leaflet, brochure
el **fondo**	bottom
al **fondo (de)**	at the bottom (of)
hacer **footing**	to go jogging
en **forma**	fit, in shape
la **forma**	shape
el **formulario**	form (to fill in)
la **foto**	photo
la **fotografía**	photography
la **frambuesa**	raspberry
francés/francesa	French
el **francés**	French (language)
el **francés**	French person (male)
la **francesa**	French person (female)
Francia	France
la **frase**	sentence, phrase
frecuentar	to hang around
frecuente	frequent
el **fregadero**	sink
fregar	to wash up
fregar los platos	to wash the dishes
la **frente**	forehead
la **fresa**	strawberry
(hace) **fresco**	(it's) cool
el **figorífico**	fridge
friego los platos	I wash the dishes
los **frijoles volteados**	fried beans
frío	cold
el **frío**	cold
la **frontera**	border
la **fruta**	fruit
la **frutería**	fruit stall, greengrocer's
fue	he/she/it was/went, you were/wen (*usted*, formal)
el **fuego**	fire
los **fuegos artificiales**	fireworks
fuera (de)	outside
fueron	they were, went
fuerte	strong, loud

■ = masculine noun ■ = feminine noun ■ = verb ■ = adjec

	Fuerteventura	Fuerteventura
la	**fuga**	flight, escape
	fui	I was, went
	fumar	to smoke
	furioso	furious
el	**fútbol**	football
el	**futbolín**	table football
el	**futbolista**	footballer (male)
la	**futbolista**	footballer (female)
el	**futuro**	future

A B C D E F G H I J K L M N O P Q R S T U V W X Y Z

Gg

las	gafas	glasses
las	gafas (de sol)	(sun)glasses
las	gaitas	bagpipes
	Gales	Wales
el	galés	Welsh (language)
	galés/galesa	Welsh
la	galleta	biscuit
la	gamba	prawn
el	ganador	winner (male)
la	ganadora	winner (female)
	ganar	to win, to earn
	ganarse la vida	to earn a living
la	ganga	bargain
	ganó	he/she/it won, you won (*usted*, formal)
el	garaje	garage
los	garbanzos	chickpeas
la	garganta	throat
el	gas	gas
la	gaseosa	lemonade
	gastar	to spend, to waste
el	gato	cat
el	gel de ducha	shower gel
la	gemela	twin (female)
el	gemelo	twin (male)
	generalmente	usually
	generoso	generous
	genial	funny
la	gente	people
la	geografía	geography
la	gimnasia	gymnastics
el	gimnasio	gymnasium
el	giro	tour
la	glorieta	roundabout
el	gobierno	government
el	gol	goal
el	golf	golf
las	golosinas	sweets
el	golpe	hit
	golpear	to hit
la	goma	eraser, rubber
	gordo	fat
el	Gordo	Christmas Eve lottery jackpot

■ = masculine noun ■ = feminine noun ■ = verb ■ = adjectiv

la	**gorra**	cap, hat
el	**gorrito**	little cap, bonnet
	grabar	to record (music)
	gracias	thank you
dar las	**gracias**	to thank
las	**gracias**	thanks
	gracias a	thanks to
	gracioso	funny, amusing
el	**gráfico**	chart, graph
el	**gramo**	gram
	Gran Bretaña	Great Britain
	grande	big
las	**grandes almacenes**	department stores
el	**granizo**	hail
la	**granja**	farm
	grasiento	greasy
	gratuito	free (no cost)
	grave	serious
	Grecia	Greece
	griego	Greek
la	**gripe**	flu
	gris	grey
	gritar	to shout
el	**grito**	cry, scream
el	**grupo**	group
el	**guacamole**	Mexican dish containing mashed avocado
el	**guante**	glove
	guapo	good-looking, beautiful, handsome
	guardar	to keep
	Guatemala	Guatemala
	guatemalteco	Guatemalan
la	**guerra**	war
el	**guerrillero**	freedom fighter
la	**guía**	guide
los	**guisantes**	peas
la	**guitarra (eléctrica)**	(electric) guitar
le	**gusta**	he/she likes it
no le	**gusta**	he/she doesn't like it
(me)	**gusta**	I like it
me	**gusta la leche**	I like milk
¿te	**gusta(n) ...?**	do you like ...? (*tú*, informal)
	gustar	to please, to like
me	**gustaría ...**	I would like ...
¿te	**gustaría ...?**	would you like? (*tú*, informal)

A B C D E F **G** H I J K L M N O P Q R S T U V W X Y Z

Hh

	haber	to have (auxiliary verb)
	había	there was/were
la	**habitación**	(bed)room
el	**habitante**	inhabitant
	habla	he/she/it speaks, you speak (*usted*, formal)
se	**habla**	they speak
	hablar	to speak
	hablar por teléfono	to talk on the telephone
	hablo	I speak
	hace buen tiempo	it's nice weather
	hace calor	it's hot
	hace deporte	he/she does sport
me	**hace falta**	I need
	hace fresco	it's chilly/cool
	hace frío	it's cold
	hace la cama	he/she makes the bed
	hace los deberes	he/she does his/her homework
	hace mal tiempo	it's bad weather
	hacer	to do/make
	hacer falta	to be needed, lacking
	hacer la compra	to do the shopping, to go shopping
	haces (los deberes)	you do (your homework) (*tú*, informal)
	hace sol	it's sunny
	hace viento	it's windy
	hacia	towards
	hago	I do
	hago deporte	I do sport
	hago la cama	I make the bed
	hago la compra	I do the shopping
	hago los deberes	I do my homework
no	**hago nada**	I don't do anything
	hago surfing	I go surfing
	hago windsurf(ing)	I go windsurfing
la	**hambre**	hunger
tengo	**hambre**	I'm hungry
la	**hamburguesa**	hamburger
el	**hámster**	hamster
la	**harina**	flour
	hasta	until
	hasta la vista	see you soon

■ = masculine noun ■ = feminine noun ■ = verb ■ = adjectiv

	hasta luego	bye, see you soon/later
	hay …	there is/are …
	¿hay…?	is/are there…?
	hay niebla	it's foggy
	hay tormenta	it's stormy
	haz	make (up) (*tú* command)
la	**heladería**	ice cream parlour
el	**helado**	ice cream
	helar	to freeze
la	**hembra**	female
la	**herida**	injury
la	**hermana**	sister
la	**hermana pequeña**	younger sister
la	**hermanastra**	stepsister
el	**hermanastro**	stepbrother
el	**hermano**	brother
el	**hermano pequeño**	younger brother
los	**hermanos**	brothers and sisters/brothers
los	**hermanos pequeños**	younger brothers and sisters/brothers
	hermoso	pretty, beautiful
	he terminado	I've finished
	hiciste	you did (*tú*, informal)
el	**hielo**	ice
la	**hierba**	grass
el	**hierro**	iron
la	**hija**	daughter
la	**hija única**	only child (girl)
el	**hijo**	son
el	**hijo único**	only child (boy)
	hispano	hispanic
la	**historia**	story
	histórico	historic
el	**hockey**	hockey
el	**hogar**	home
sin	**hogar**	homeless
	hola	hello, hi
el	**hombre**	man
	Honduras	Honduras
	hondureño	Honduran
a la	**hora**	on time
la	**hora**	the time, hour
la	**hora de comer**	lunchtime
¿qué	**hora es?**	what time is it?
el	**horario**	timetable
el	**horno**	oven

■ = masculine noun ■ = feminine noun ■ = verb ■ = adjective

A B C D E F G H I J K L M N O P Q R S T U V W X Y Z

horrible	horrible
el hospital	hospital
el hotel	hotel
hoy	today
el hueco	gap
la huerta	vegetable garden
el hueso	bone
el huevo	egg
humano	human
el humo	smoke
el humor	humour

= masculine noun = feminine noun = verb = adjective

Ii

	iba	I used to go
	Ibiza	Ibiza
buena	idea	good idea
la	idea	idea
la	identificación	identification
	identificar	to identify
el	idioma	language
	IES (Instituto de Enseñanza Secundaria)	secondary school
la	iglesia	church
	igual	equal, the same
me es	igual	I don't mind
la	imagen	image
la	imaginación	imagination
	imaginar	to imagine
	imaginativo	imaginative
	imitar	to imitate
	impaciente	impatient
el	impermeable	raincoat
no	importa	it doesn't matter
	importante	important
la	impresora	printer
	imprime	print (*tú* command)
	imprimir	to print
	inalámbrico	cordless
	incluir	to include
	incluye	include (*tú* command)
	incómodo	uncomfortable
	increíble	incredible
	indica	indicate, point to (*tú* command)
	indicar	to indicate
	indígeno	native, indigenous
	indio	Indian
	industrial	industrial
	infantil	childish
la	información	information
	informar	to report
la	informática	information technology, ICT
la	ingeniera	engineer (female)
el	ingeniero	engineer (male)
	Inglaterra	England
	inglés/inglesa	English

■ = masculine noun ■ = feminine noun ■ = verb ■ = adjective

A B C D E F G H I J K L M N O P Q R S T U V W X Y Z

el	inglés	English (language)
el	inglés	English person (male)
la	inglesa	English person (female)
el	ingrediente	ingredient
	inmediatamente	immediately
	inmóvil	still
el	insecto	insect
la	insolación	sunstroke
el	instituto	school, institute, secondary school
el	instituto femenino	girls' school
el	instituto masculino	boys' school
el	instituto mixto	mixed school
la	instrucción	instruction
el	instrumento	instrument
	insuficiente	poor (mark)
	intelectual	intellectual
	inteligente	intelligent
el	intercambio	exchange
el	interés	interest
	interesante	interesting
	internacional	international
el	Internet	Internet
	introducir	to introduce
	inútil	useless
el	invierno	winter
la	invitación	invitation
la	invitada	guest (female)
el	invitado	guest (male)
	invitar	to invite
	ir	to go
	ir a la piscina	to go to the swimming pool
	ir al cine	to go to the cinema
	ir al polideportivo	to go to the sports centre
	ir de compras	to go shopping
	ir (de excursión)	to go (on a trip)
	Irlanda	Ireland
	Irlanda del Norte	Nothern Ireland
	irlandés/irlandesa	Irish
	irse	to go away
la	isla	island
las	Islas Baleares	Balearic Islands
las	Islas Canarias	Canary Islands
	Italia	Italy
la	italiana	Italian person (female)
	italiano	Italian

■ = masculine noun ■ = feminine noun ■ = verb ■ = adjective

el italiano	Italian person (male)
el italiano	Italian (language)
el itinerario	journey, itinerary
la izquierda	left
a la izquierda (de)	to the left (of)

A B C D E F G H I J K L M N O P Q R S T U V W X Y Z

Jj

el	jabón	soap
	Jamaica	Jamaica
	jamaicano	Jamaican
	jamás	never, ever
el	jamón	ham
el	jamón serrano	Parma ham
el	jarabe	syrup
el	jardín	garden
el	jardinero	gardener
la	jaula	cage
el	jerez	sherry
el	jersey	jumper
	joven	young
el	joven	teenager (male)
la	joven	teenager (female)
la	joya	jewel
la	joyería	jeweller's
la	judía	Jew (female)
las	judías (verdes)	(green) beans
	judío	Jewish
el	judío	Jew (male)
el	judo	judo
	juega a las cartas	he/she plays cards
	juegan	they play
	juego	I play
el	juego	game
los	Juegos Olímpicos	Olympic Games
(el)	jueves	(on) Thursday
	jugar	to play (game)
	jugar con el ordenador	to play on the computer
	jugar con los videojuegos	to play video games
	jugar con mi PlayStation	to play with my PlayStation
	jugaron	they/you played (*ustedes*, formal)
	jugó	he/she/you played (*usted*, formal)
	jugué	I played
el	juguete	toy
	julio	July
	junio	June
	junto a	next to
	juntos	together, side by side
	justo	just, fair
	juvenil	for young people

■ = masculine noun ■ = feminine noun ■ = verb ■ = adjectiv

Kk

el	**kilo**	kilo
el	**kilómetro**	kilometre

A B C D E F G H I J K L M N O P Q R S T U V W X Y Z

Ll

	la	the
el	**labio**	lip
el	**laboratorio**	laboratory
el	**laboratorio de idiomas**	language lab(oratory)
al	**lado (de)**	beside, next to
el	**lago**	lake
la	**lámpara**	lamp
de	**lana**	made of wool
la	**lana**	wool
	Lanzarote	Lanzarote
el	**lapicero**	pencil
el	**lápiz**	pencil
	largo	long
	las	the
la	**lástima**	pity
la	**lata**	tin
el	**lavabo**	sink, washbasin
la	**lavadora**	washing machine
la	**lavandería**	laundry
	lavar/lavarse	to wash/to wash oneself
	lavar el coche	to wash the car
te	**lavas los dientes**	you brush your teeth (*tú*, informal)
	lavo el coche	I wash the car
la	**leche**	milk
la	**lechuga**	lettuce
la	**lechuza**	owl
	lee	read (*tú* command)
	leer	to read
los	**legumbres**	vegetables
	leí	I read
	lejos (de)	far (from)
la	**lengua**	tongue, language
el	**lenguaje**	(study of) language
	lentamente	slowly
la	**lente de contacto**	contact lens
las	**lentejas**	lentils
	lento	slow
el	**leopardo**	leopard
la	**letra**	letter
el	**letrero**	sign
se	**levanta**	he/she gets up
	levantaos	stand up (*vosotros* command)

■ = masculine noun ■ = feminine noun ■ = verb ■ = adjecti

	levantar	to lift
	levantarse	to get up
te	levantas	you get up (*tú*, informal)
(no) me	levanto	I (don't) get up
la	ley	law
la	libra (esterlina)	pound (sterling)
	libre	free
la	librería	bookshop, bookcase
el	libro	(text)book
la	lidia	bullfight
	ligar	to chat up
	ligero	light
el	limón	lemon
la	limonada	lemonade
	limpiar	to clean
	limpio	clean
la	línea	line
la	linterna	torch
	liso	straight, smooth
la	lista	register, list
	listo	ready, clever
el	litro	litre
la	llama	llama
se	llama ...	his/her/its name is ... , your name is ... (*usted*, formal)
se	llaman ...	their names are ..., your names are ... (*ustedes*, formal)
	llamar	to call
	llamar por teléfono	to telephone
	llamarse	to be called
me	llamo ...	my name is ...
	llano	flat
la	llave	key
el	llavero	key ring
	llega	he/she/it arrives, comes, you arrive, come (*usted*, formal)
	llega a casa	he/she arrives home
	llegáis a casa	you arrive home (*vosotros*)
	llegar	to arrive
	llego	I come, arrive
	llego a casa	I arrive home
	llego a pie	I walk
	llenar	to fill up
	lleno	full
	llevar	to carry, wear

A B C D E F G H I J K **L** M N O P Q R S T U V W X Y Z

= masculine noun = feminine noun = verb = adjective

A B C D E F G H I J K L M N O P Q R S T U V W X Y Z

	llevar al perro	to take the dog for a walk
	llevarse bien/mal (con)	to get on well/badly (with)
	llevo	I wear, I've got
	llorar	to cry
	llover	to rain
	llueve	it's raining
la	**lluvia**	rain
	loco	mad
	Londres	London
el	**loro**	parrot
	los	the
	lo siento	I'm sorry
la	**lotería**	lottery
la	**lucha**	fight
	luchar	to fight
	luego	then, next
desde	**luego**	of course
(hasta)	**luego**	(see you) later/soon
el	**lugar**	place
la	**luna**	moon
(el)	**lunes**	(on) Monday
la	**luz**	light

■ = masculine noun ■ = feminine noun ■ = verb ■ = adjectiv

Mm

el	macho	male
la	madera	wood
la	madrastra	stepmother
la	madre	mother
la	magdalena	Spanish cupcake
	mágico	magic
el	magnetofón	tape recorder
	magnífico	magnificent
el	maíz	corn
	majo	nice
	mal	unhappy, unwell
la	maleta	suitcase
	malísimo	very bad
	Mallorca	Majorca
	mallorquín/mallorquina	Majorcan
	malo	bad, wicked
	mamá	mum
de la	mañana	a.m.
la	mañana	morning, tomorrow
por la	mañana	in the morning
la	Mancha	English Channel
	manchar	to stain
	mandando	sending
	mándanos	send us (*tú* command)
	mandar	to send
	mandar mensajes	to send (text) messages
la	manera	manner, way
la	manga	sleeve
la	mano	hand
la	manteca	animal fat
	mantener	to maintain, to keep
la	mantequilla	butter
las	manualidades	crafts
la	manzana	apple
el	mapa	map
la	máquina (fotográfica)	camera
el	mar	sea
	marca	mark (*tú* command)
	marcar	to dial, to mark
	marcar un gol	to score a goal
estar	mareado	to feel sick
el	marido	husband

= masculine noun = feminine noun = verb = adjective

A B C D E F G H I J K L **M** N O P Q R S T U V W X Y Z

los	**mariscos**	seafood
	marrón	brown
el	**martes**	(on) Tuesday
	marzo	March
	más	more, most
la	**máscara**	mask
la	**mascota**	pet
	masculino	masculine
	más de	more than
	matar	to kill
las	**matemáticas**	maths
el	**matrimonio**	marriage
	maya	Mayan
	mayo	May
	mayor	older, greater, elder
	me	(to) me
la	**mecánica**	mechanic (female)
el	**mecánico**	mechanic (male)
la	**media hora**	half an hour
	mediano	medium-sized
la	**medianoche**	midnight
las	**medias**	tights
la	**médica**	doctor (female)
la	**medicina**	medicine
el	**médico**	doctor (male)
	medio	half
el	**medio ambiente**	environment
el	**mediodía**	midday
	medir	to measure
	mediterráneo	Mediterranean
el	**Mediterráneo**	the Mediterranean
	mejicano	Mexican
	Méjico	Mexico
	mejor	best
	mejorar	to improve
el	**melocotón**	peach
la	**memoria**	memory
se	**menciona**	it is mentioned
	mencionado	mentioned
se	**mencionan**	are mentioned
	mencionar	to mention
	menor	younger
	Menorca	Minorca
	menorquín/menorquina	Minorcan
	menos	minus

■ = masculine noun ■ = feminine noun ■ = verb ■ = adjecti

el	**mensaje**	(text) message
	mensualmente	monthly
	mentira	false
la	**mentira**	lie
el	**menú**	menu
el	**mercado**	market
	merendar	to have an afternoon snack
la	**merienda**	afternoon snack, picnic
	meriendas	you have tea (*tú*, informal)
	meriendo	I have tea
la	**merluza**	hake
la	**mermelada**	jam, marmalade
el	**mes**	month
la	**mesa**	table
la	**mesa del profesor**	teacher's desk
la	**mesilla**	bedside table
la	**mesita**	bedside table
la	**meta**	goal, aim
el	**metal**	metal
	meter	to put
el	**metro**	metre, underground
en	**metro**	by underground train
	mexicano	Mexican
	México	Mexico
	mezclar	to mix
la	**mezquita**	mosque
	mi	my (singular)
	mí	me
el	**micrófono**	microphone
el	**microondas**	microwave oven
el	**miedo**	fear
la	**miel**	honey
el	**miembro**	member
	mientras	meanwhile, whilst
(el)	**miércoles**	(on) Wednesday
	mil	a thousand
el	**milenio**	millennium
la	**mili**	military service
el	**millón**	million
el	**minuto**	minute
	mío	mine
	mira	look (*tú* command)
	mirad ...	look at ... (*vosotros* command)
	mirar	to look at
	mis	my (plural)

A B C D E F G H I J K L M N O P Q R S T U V W X Y Z

la misa	mass
la misa del gallo	midnight mass
mismo	same
el misterio	mystery
la mitad	half
la mochila	school bag, rucksack
de moda	fashionable
fuera de moda	not fashionable
la moda	fashion
pasado de moda	old-fashioned
el modelo	model
moderno	new, modern
mojado	wet
de momento	at the moment
el momento	moment
la moneda	coin
el monedero	purse
el monitor	monitor (TV, computer)
el mono	monkey
el monopatín	skateboard
la montaña	mountain
montar	to ride
montar a caballo	to go horse riding
monto en bicicleta	I ride my bicycle
monto en monopatín	I go skateboarding
el monumento	monument, site
morado	purple
moreno	dark (hair, skin)
morir	to die
la mosca	fly
Moscú	Moscow
la mostaza	mustard
mostrar	to show
en moto	by motorbike
la moto	motorbike
el motor	motor
mover	to move, to stir
móvil	mobile
el móvil	mobile phone
muchas veces	often
mucho	a lot, lots of
mudarse	to move house
los muebles	furniture
las muelas	(back) teeth
muerto	dead

	mueva	move (*usted* command)
	mueve	move (*tú* command)
	muévete	move yourself (*tú* command)
la	**mujer**	woman, wife
	multicolor	multicoloured
el	**mundo**	world
el	**músculo**	muscle
el	**museo**	museum
la	**música**	musician (female)
la	**música (pop)**	(pop) music
el	**músico**	musician (male)
	musulmán/musulmana	Muslim
	muy	very
	muy bien	very well

A B C D E F G H I J K L M **N** O P Q R S T U V W X Y Z

Nn

	nacer	to be born
	naciendo	being born
el	**nacimiento**	birth
	nacional	national
la	**nacionalidad**	nationality
	nada	nothing
	nada más	nothing else
	nadar	to swim
	nadie	nobody, no one
color	**naranja**	orange (colour)
la	**naranja**	orange
la	**naranjada**	orangeade
la	**nariz**	nose
la	**nata**	cream
la	**natación**	swimming
la	**naturaleza**	nature
	naturalmente	of course
	navegar por Internet	to surf the Internet
la	**Navidad**	Christmas
	necesario	necessary
	necesitan	they/you need (*ustedes*, formal)
	necesitar	to need
	necesitas	you need (*tú*, informal)
	necesito	I need
	negativo	negative
el	**negocio**	business, firm
los	**negocios**	business, trade
	negro	black
	neozelandés/ neozelandesa	from New Zealand
	nervioso	nervous
	nevar	to snow
la	**nevera**	fridge
	ni ... ni ...	neither ... nor ...
	Nicaragua	Nicaragua
	nicaragüense	Nicaraguan
el	**nido**	nest
la	**niebla**	fog
la	**nieta**	granddaughter
el	**nieto**	grandson
	nieva	it's snowing
la	**nieve**	snow

■ = masculine noun ■ = feminine noun ■ = verb ■ = adjectiv

	Nigeria	Nigeria
	nigeriano	Nigerian
la	**niña**	child (female)
	ningún, ninguna	no, none
el	**niño**	child (male)
el	**nivel**	level
	no	no
la	**noche**	night
por la	**noche**	at night
la	**Nochebuena**	Christmas Eve
la	**Nochevieja**	New Year's Eve
	nocturno	night
el	**nombre**	name
el	**noreste**	north-east
la	**norma**	rule, regulation
	normalmente	normally, usually
el	**noroeste**	north-west
el	**norte**	north
al	**norte de ...**	to the north of
	nosotros	we, us
la	**nota**	mark (school) note
	notable	very good
las	**noticias**	news
	no ... todavía	not yet
	novecientos	nine hundred
	noveno	ninth
	noventa	ninety
la	**novia**	girlfriend
	noviembre	November
el	**novio**	boyfriend
la	**nube**	cloud
	nublado	cloudy
	nuestro/a	our
	nueve	nine
	Nueva Zelanda	New Zealand
	nuevo	new
el	**número**	number
el	**número de identidad**	identity number
	nunca	never
	nutritivo	nutritious

A B C D E F G H I J K L M N O P Q R S T U V W X Y Z

A B C D E F G H I J K L M N **O** P Q R S T U V W X Y Z

Oo

	o	or
el	**objetivo**	objective
el	**objeto**	object
los	**objetos perdidos**	lost property
	obligatorio	obligatory
la	**obra**	work (of art)
	octavo	eighth
	obtener	to get, to obtain
	obvio	obvious
el	**océano**	ocean
	ochenta	eighty
	ocho	eight
	octubre	October
	ocupado	busy
	odia	he/she hates, you hate (*usted*, formal)
	odiar	to hate
	odio	I hate
el	**oeste**	west
la	**oferta**	special offer
	oficial	official
la	**oficina**	office
la	**oficina de turismo**	tourist office
el	**oído**	ear
	oír	to hear
	¡ojalá!	I wish!, if only!
	¡ojo!	watch out!
el	**ojo**	eye
el	**ojo morado**	black eye
la	**ola**	wave
	oler	to smell
la	**oliva**	olive
el	**olor**	smell
	ondulado	wavy
la	**opción**	option
	opinar (de)	to think (of)
	opinas	you think (*tú*, informal)
en mi	**opinión**	in my opinion
la	**opinión**	opinion
	opuesto	opposite
el	**orden**	order
el	**ordenador**	computer
la	**oreja**	ear

■ = masculine noun ■ = feminine noun ■ = verb ■ = adjective

	orgánico	organic
la	organización	organisation
	orgulloso	proud
el	origen	origin
la	orilla	shore, river bank
el	oro	gold
la	ortografía	spelling
	oscuro	dark
el	otoño	autumn
	otra vez	again
	otro	another, other
la	oveja	sheep
el	oxígeno	oxygen
	oye	listen (*tú* command)
el	ozono	ozone

Pp

el paciente	patient (male)
la paciente	patient (female)
el padrastro	stepfather
el padre	father
los padres	parents, fathers
la paella	paella
pagar	to pay
la página	page
el país	country
el paisaje	countryside, landscape
los Países Bajos	the Netherlands
el País Vasco	Basque Country
el pájaro	bird
la palabra	word
el palacio	palace
la Palma	Palma
el palo	stick
la paloma	dove, pigeon
las palomitas de maíz	popcorn
el pan	bread
la panadería	baker's
el pañal	nappy
Panamá	Panama
la pandilla	group of friends
la pantalla	screen
el pantalón	trousers
el pantalón corto	shorts
los pantalones vaqueros	jeans
el pan tostado	toast
papá	dad
el papel	paper
la papelera	bin
el paquete	packet, parcel
Paquistán	Pakistan
paquistaní	Pakistani
el par	pair
para	for, in order to
la parada	stop
la parada de autobús	bus stop
parado	unemployed
el paraguas	umbrella

■ = masculine noun ■ = feminine noun ■ = verb ■ = adjective

	Paraguay	Paraguay
el	parapente	paragliding
	parar	to switch off (engine)
	parar(se)	to stop
	parecerse	to look like
	parecido	similar
el	parecido	similarity
la	pared	wall
el	pariente	relation, relative (male)
la	pariente	relation, relative (female)
el	parlamento	parliament
el	paro	unemployment
el	parque	park
el	parque de atracciones	funfair
el	parque nacional	national park
el	parque temático	theme park
el	párrafo	paragraph
en alguna	parte	somewhere
la	parte	part
	participar	to participate
en	particular	in particular
el	partido	match
el	partido de fútbol	football match
el	pasado	the past
	pasado de moda	old-fashioned
	pasado mañana	the day after tomorrow
la	pasajera	passenger (female)
el	pasajero	passenger (male)
el	pasaporte	passport
	pasar	to spend (time), to happen, to pass
	pasar la aspiradora	to hoover
	pasarlo bien/bomba/mal	to have a good/great/bad time
el	pasatiempo	hobby, pastime
la	Pascua	Easter
	pasearse	to go for a walk
el	paseo	walk, avenue, boulevard
el	pasillo	corridor, hallway
el	paso	step
	paso la aspiradora	I hoover
la	pasta	pasta
la	pasta de dientes	toothpaste
el	pastel	cake
la	pastelería	cake shop
la	pastilla	pill, tablet
las	patatas fritas	chips, crisps

A B C D E F G H I J K L M N O **P** Q R S T U V W X Y Z

= masculine noun ■ = feminine noun ■ = verb ■ = adjective

A B C D E F G H I J K L M N O **P** Q R S T U V W X Y Z

el	patinaje	skating
	patinar	to skate
	patinar sobre hielo	to ice skate
el	patín de hielo	ice skate
el	patio	playground, patio
el	pavo	turkey
la	paz	peace
la	peca	freckle
el	pececito	goldfish
los	peces	fishes
el	pedazo	piece, slice
	pedir	to ask for
el	pegamento	glue
	peinarse	to comb/brush one's hair
te	peinas	you comb/brush your hair (*tú*, informal)
el	peine	comb
me	peino	I comb/brush my hair
	pelar	to peel
la	película	film
la	película de guerra	war film
la	película del oeste	western film
la	película policíaca	thriller film
el	peligro	danger
	peligroso	dangerous
	pelirrojo	red-haired, red-headed
el	penique	penny
el	pelo	hair
la	pelota	ball, pelota (game)
la	peluche	cuddly toy
la	peluquera	hairdresser (female)
la	peluquería	hairdresser's
el	peluquero	hairdresser (male)
	pensar (en)	to think (about)
la	pensión	guest house
el	pensionista	OAP (male)
la	pensionista	OAP (female)
	peor	worse
	pequeño	small
	perder	to lose
	perezoso	lazy
	perfecto	perfect
la	perfumería	perfume shop
el	periódico	newspaper
el	periodista	journalist (male)

■ = masculine noun ■ = feminine noun ■ = verb ■ = adjecti

la	periodista	journalist (female)
	permitir	to allow, to permit
	pero	but
el	perrito caliente	hot dog
el	perro	dog
llevar al	perro	to walk the dog
la(s)	persiana(s)	blind(s)
la	persona	person
el	personaje	famous person, character
	personal	personal
	Perú	Peru
	pesado	heavy
	pesar	to weigh
la	pesca	fishing
la	pescadería	fishmonger's
el	pescado	fish
el	pescador	fisherman
	pescar	to fish
la	pestaña	eyelash
el	pez (de colores)	(gold) fish
el	piano	piano
la	picadura	insect bite
	picante	spicy
	picar	to sting
a	pie	on foot
el	pie	foot
la	piedra	stone
la	piel	skin
	pienso que ...	I think that
la	pierna	leg
	pijo	posh
el	piloto	pilot
la	pimienta	pepper (spice)
el	pimiento	(sweet) pepper
	pintar	to paint
la	pintura	painting
el	piragüismo	canoeing
los	Pirineos	Pyrenees
la	piscina	swimming pool
el	piso	flat, floor
la	pista	course
la	pista de hielo	ice rink
la	pista de tenis	tennis court
la	pista polideportivo	sports pitch
la	piza	chalk

= masculine noun = feminine noun = verb = adjective

A B C D E F G H I J K L M N O **P** Q R S T U V W X Y Z

la	**pizarra**	blackboard, whiteboard
la	**pizza**	pizza
el	**plan**	plan
	planchar	to iron
	plancho	I do the ironing
el	**planeta**	planet
la	**planta**	plant
la	**planta (baja)**	(ground) floor
la	**plantación**	plantation
	plantar	to plant
el	**plástico**	plastic
la	**plata**	silver
el	**plátano**	banana
el	**plato**	plate
la	**playa**	beach
la	**plaza**	square
la	**plaza de toros**	bullring
la	**plaza mayor**	the main square
la	**pluma**	(fountain) pen
las	**plumas**	feathers
la	**población**	population
	pobre	poor, unfortunate
	poco	little, not much
un	**poco**	a little
	poder	to be able
	poderoso	powerful
la	**poesía**	poem
el	**policía**	policeman
la	**policía**	policewoman
el	**polideportivo**	sports centre
el	**pollo**	chicken
el	**polo**	pole (North/South), polo shirt
la	**polución**	pollution
la	**pomada**	cream, ointment
el	**pomelo**	grapefruit
	pon	put (*tú* command)
	poner	to put (on)
	poner la mesa	to lay the table
	ponerse	to put on (clothes), to wear
	ponerse de pie	to stand up
	ponerse moreno	to get a tan
	pongo la mesa	I lay the table
	popular	popular
	por	for
	por aquí	nearby

■ = masculine noun ■ = feminine noun ■ = verb ■ = adjecti

la	porción	portion
	¿por dónde se va a ...?	which way is it to ...?
	por ejemplo	for example
	por favor	please
	por la mañana/tarde	in the morning/afternoon
	por la noche	at night
	¿por qué?	why?
	porque	because
	por supuesto	of course
	portátil	portable
	Portugal	Portugal
	portugués/portuguesa	Portuguese
la	posibilidad	possibility
	posible	possible
	posiblemente	possibly
la	posición	position
la	postal	postcard
el	póster	poster
el	postre	dessert
la	práctica	practice
	practicar	to practise, to do (a sport)
	práctico	practical
	practico el deporte	I do sport
el	precio	price
	precioso	beautiful
	prefiero	I prefer
el	prefijo	dialling code
la	pregunta	question
	preguntar	to ask a question
el	premio	prize
	preocupado	worried
	preocuparse	to worry
la	preparación	preparation
	preparar la cena	to prepare supper/dinner
	prepararse	to get ready
	preparo la cena	I prepare supper/dinner
el	presentador	presenter (male)
la	presentadora	presenter (female)
	presentar	to present, to introduce
	prestar	to lend
la	prima	cousin (female)
la	primavera	spring
la	primera	the first
	primero	first of all
	primero	first

A B C D E F G H I J K L M N O **P** Q R S T U V W X Y Z

el	primero de (mayo)	the first of (May)
el	primer piso	first floor
el	primo	cousin (male)
	principal	main
el	principio	beginning, principle
tener	prisa	to be in a hurry
	privado	private
	probar	to try
el	problema	problem
	producir	to produce
el	producto	product
la	profesión	profession
	profesional	professional
el	profesor	teacher (male)
la	profesora	teacher (female)
el	programa de televisión	television programme
el	progreso	progress
	prohibido	forbidden
el	pronóstico	forecast
	pronto	early
	pronto	ready, early
hasta	pronto	see you soon
la	pronunciación	pronunciation
	pronunciar	to pronounce
	propio	own
los buenos	propósitos de fin de año	New Year's resolutions
la	protección	protection
	proteger	to protect
la	proteína	protein
	próximo	next, close
la	prueba	test
el	público	the public
el	pueblo	small town, village
se	puede	one/you can
	puedes	you can (*tú*, informal)
	¿puedes repetir?	can you repeat that? (*tú*, informal)
el	puente	bridge
la	puerta	door, gate
el	puerto	port
	puertorriqueño	Puerto Rican
	pues	well
	pulsar	to click on (computer)
el	punto	dot
en	punto	exactly, precisely (time)
	puntual	on time

= masculine noun = feminine noun = verb = adjecti

Qq

	que	which, that, who
	¿qué?	what?
	¡qué bien!	how nice!
	quedar (a)	to fit
	quedar (con)	to meet
	quedar(se)	to stay, to remain
	¿qué dice ...?	what does ... say?
	¿qué es ...?	what is (it)?
	¿qué haces?	what do you do? (*tú*, informal)
	¿qué hay ...?	what is there ...?
	¿qué hora es?	what time is it?
	¿qué idiomas hablas?	what languages do you speak? (*tú*, informal)
la	**queja**	complaint
	querer	to want
	querer decir	to mean
	querido	dear
el	**queso**	cheese
	¿qué son?	what are (they)?
	¿qué tal?	how are things?
	¿qué te gusta hacer?	what do you like doing? (*tú*, informal)
	¿qué tiempo hace?	what's the weather like?
	¿qué tiene ...?	what does ... have?
	¿qué vas a hacer?	what are you going to do? (*tú*, informal)
el	**quiche**	Guatemalan language
	¿quién?	who?
	quiere	he/she wants, you want (*usted*, formal)
	quieren	they, you want (*ustedes*, formal)
	quieres	you want (*tú*, informal)
	¿quieres ...?	do you want ... ? (*tú*, informal)
	¿quieres ir al cine?	do you want to go to the cinema?
	¿quieres jugar al tenis?	do you want to play tennis?
	¿quieres salir?	do you want to go out?
	quiero	I want, I would like
te	**quiero**	I love you
la	**química**	chemistry
	quince	fifteen
	quince días	fortnight
	quinientos	five hundred
las	**quintillizas**	quintuplets (female)

A B C D E F G H I J K L M N O P **Q** R S T U V W X Y Z

los	**quintillizos**	quintuplets (male)
	quinto	fifth
el	**quiosco**	kiosk
	quisiera	I wish, I would like
	quitar el polvo (a)	to dust
	quitar la mesa	to clear the table
	quitar(se)	to take away, to take off
	quito la mesa	I clear the table
	quizá(s)	perhaps

Rr

la	ración	portion
el	racismo	racism
el	radiador	radiator
la	radio	radio
la	radiografía	X-ray
	rapado	close cropped/shaven
	rápido	quick, fast
la	raqueta	racket (tennis)
el	rasgo	slash
la	rata	rat
el	ratón	mouse (animal, computer)
los	ratos libres	free moments
	rayado	striped
la	razón	reason
	real	royal
en	realidad	in fact
	realizar	to realise, to fulfil
la	rebaja	reduction
la	receta	recipe, prescription
	recibir	to receive
el	recibo	receipt
el	reciclaje	recycling
	reciclar	to recycle
	reciente	recent
	recoger	to collect, to tidy up, to pick up
	recogido	quiet, reserved
la	recomendación	recommendation
	recomendar	to recommend
	recomienda	he/she recommends, you recommend (*usted*, formal)
	recordar(se)	to remember
el	recreo	break, playtime
	recto	straight
el	recuerdo	souvenir
	recuerdos	regards (in a letter)
la	red	network
	redondo	round
la	reducción	reduction
	reducir	to reduce
	reformado	altered
el	refrán	chorus
el	refresco	soft drink

A B C D E F G H I J K L M N O P Q R S T U V W X Y Z

el	regalo	present
la	región	region
	registrar	to record (computer)
la	regla	ruler, rule
	regresar	to go back, to return
	regular	so-so, alright
	regularmente	regularly
la	reina	queen
el	Reino Unido	the United Kingdom
la	relación	relationship
	relajado	relaxed
	relajante	relaxing
la	religión	religion, RE
	rellenar	to fill in (form)
el	reloj	clock, watch
	RENFE (Red Nacional de los Ferrocarriles Españoles)	Spanish railway network
	reparar	to repair
	repasar	to revise
de	repente	suddenly
	repetir	to repeat
	repite	repeat (*tú*, command)
la	República Dominicana	the Dominican Republic
estar	resfriado	to have a cold
el	requesón	cottage cheese
	reservado	shy, reserved
	reservar	to reserve, to book
	respirar	to breathe
	responder	to answer
la	respuesta	answer
el	restaurante	restaurant
el	resultado	result
el	resumen	summary
la	revista	magazine
el	rey	king
los	Reyes Magos	the Three Kings
Costa	Rica	Costa Rica
	rico	rich, delicious
el	riesgo	risk
el	rincón	corner
el	río	river
	rizado	curly
	robar	to steal
la	roca	rock

■ = masculine noun ■ = feminine noun ■ = verb ■ = adjecti

la	**rodilla**	knee
	rojo	red, ginger (hair)
	romano	Roman
	romántico	romantic
	romper	to break
	roncar	to snore
la	**ropa**	clothing, clothes
	rosa	pink
	roto	broken
el	**rotulador**	felt-tip pen
	rubio	fair, fair-haired
la	**rueda**	wheel
el	**rugby**	rugby
el	**ruido**	noise
	ruidoso	noisy
	ruso	Russian
la	**ruta**	route
la	**rutina**	routine
la	**rutina diaria**	daily routine

A B C D E F G H I J K L M N O P Q R S T U V W X Y Z

A B C D E F G H I J K L M N O P Q R **S** T U V W X Y Z

Ss

	Spanish	English
(el)	**sábado**	(on) Saturday
	saber	to know (about something)
el	**sabor**	taste, flavour
el	**sacapuntas**	pencil sharpener
	sacar	to take out
	sacar la basura	(to) put the rubbish out
el	**saco de dormir**	sleeping bag
	saco la basura	I put the rubbish out
la	**sal**	salt
la	**sala**	(sitting) room
la	**sala de actos**	hall
la	**sala (de juegos)**	(games) room
la	**sala de profesores**	staffroom
la	**salchicha**	sausage
	sal del sistema	log off (*tú* command)
los	**saldos**	sales
	salgo con amigos	I go out with friends
la	**salida**	exit, way out
	salir	to go out, leave
	salir con amigos	to go out with friends
	salir del sistema	to log off
	salir en balandro	to go sailing
el	**salmón**	salmon
el	**salón**	living room
el	**salón comedor**	lounge-diner
la	**salsa**	sauce
	saltar	to jump
el	**salto**	jump
la	**salud**	health, fitness
	saludar	to greet
	saludos	regards, best wishes (in a letter)
El	**Salvador**	El Salvador
	salvadoreño	Salvadorean
	salvaje	wild
	salvar	to save
la	**sandalia**	sandal
	sano	healthy
la	**sardina**	sardine
no	**sé**	I don't know
	seco	dry
la	**secretaria**	secretary (female)
el	**secretario**	secretary (male)

■ = masculine noun ■ = feminine noun ■ = verb ■ = adjectiv

	secreto	secret
la	sed	thirst
tengo	sed	I'm thirsty
la	seda	silk
en	seguida	straight away, immediately
	seguir	to continue, to follow
	según	according to
la	segunda	the second
de	segunda mano	second-hand
	segundo	second
	seguro	sure, safe, certain
	seis	six
el	sello	stamp
la	selva	forest, jungle
el	semáforo	traffic lights
la	semana	week
	semanalmente	weekly
la	Semana Santa	Holy Week, Easter
	sembrar	to sow
	señalar	to point, to signal
	sencillamente	simply
	sencillo	simple
	Señor	Mr
el	señor	gentleman
	Señora	Mrs
la	señora	lady
	Señores	Mr and Mrs
	Señorita	Miss/Ms
la	señorita	young lady
	sensible	sensitive
	sentaos	sit down (*vosotros* command)
	sentarse	to sit (down)
el	sentido	sense
	sentir(se)	to feel
	separar	to separate
	septiembre, setiembre	September
	séptimo	seventh
la	sequía	dry period, drought
	ser	to be
la	serie	series
	serio	serious
la	serpiente	snake
los	servicios	toilets
	sesenta	sixty
la	sesión	showing (cinema)

■ = masculine noun ■ = feminine noun ■ = verb ■ = adjective

A B C D E F G H I J K L M N O P Q R **S** T U V W X Y Z

	setecientos	seven hundred
	setenta	seventy
	setiembre, septiembre	September
	severo	strict
	sexto	sixth
	si	if
	sí	yes
el	**SIDA**	AIDS
la	**sidra**	cider
	siempre	always
lo	**siento**	I'm sorry
me	**siento**	I feel
la	**sierra**	mountains
la	**siesta**	siesta, nap
	siete	seven
	significar	to mean
	sigue	continue (*tú* command)
	siguiente	following, next
el	**silencio**	silence
la	**silla**	chair
la	**silla de ruedas**	wheel chair
el	**sillón**	armchair
	similar	similar
	simpático	nice/friendly (person)
	sin	without
	sincero	sincere, kind
	sin embargo	nevertheless, however
	sino	but
el	**síntoma**	symptom
el	**sistema**	system
el	**sitio**	site, place
el	**sitio web**	website
la	**situación**	situation
estar	**situado**	to be situated
	sobre	about, on (top of)
el	**sobre**	envelope
	sobresaliente	excellent
	sobre todo	especially, above all
la	**sobrina**	niece
el	**sobrino**	nephew
	sociable	sociable, friendly
la	**sociedad**	society
el	**socorro**	help
el	**sofá**	sofa
	sois	you are (*vosotros*)

■ = masculine noun ■ = feminine noun ■ = verb ■ = adjectiv

el **sol**	sun
hace **sol**	it's sunny
solamente	only
el **soldado**	soldier
soler	to be used to (doing), to (do) usually
solidario	caring
sólo	only
solo	alone, lonely
la **soltera**	unmarried, single person (female)
el **soltero**	unmarried, single person (male)
la **solución**	solution
el **sombrero**	hat
somos	we are
son	equals
son	they are, you are (*ustedes*, formal)
soñar	to dream
el **sondeo**	poll, questionnaire, survey
son las	it's ... o'clock
son las ... menos cuarto	it's quarter to ...
son las ... y cuarto/media	it's quarter past/half past ...
sonreír	to smile
la **sonrisa**	smile
la **sopa**	soup
sordo	deaf
sorprender	to surprise
la **sorpresa**	surprise
soso	dull
el **sótano**	basement
soy de ...	I'm from ...
soy (Pedro)	I am, I'm (Pedro)
el **squash**	squash
su	his/her/your (*usted*, formal)/their
sube (por)	go up (*tú* command)
subir	to go up, to climb
subrayar	to underline
sucio	dirty
la **sudadera**	sweatshirt
Sudamérica	South America
sudamericano	South American
el **suelo**	floor, ground
el **sueño**	dream
la **suerte**	luck
¡qué tengas **suerte**!	good luck!
la **sugerencia**	suggestion
sugerir	to suggest

la	**Suiza**	Switzerland
	suizo	Swiss
el	**supermercado**	supermarket
el	**sur**	south
el	**sureste**	south-east
el	**suroeste**	south-west
	suyo	his, hers

■ = masculine noun ■ = feminine noun ■ = verb ■ = adjectiv

Tt

el **tabaco**	tobacco
el **tablao flamenco**	flamenco show
el **taco**	filled rolled tortilla
el **tacón**	heel (of shoe)
¿qué **tal?**	how are you?
la **talla**	size (clothes)
de **talla mediana**	medium height
el **taller**	workshop
el **taller de arte**	art room
el **taller de manualidades**	crafts workshop
tal vez	perhaps
también	also, too
yo **también**	me too
el **Támesis**	the Thames
tampoco	either, neither
yo **tampoco**	me neither
tan (... como)	so, as (... as)
tanto	so much, as much
la **tapa**	snack, lid
la **taquilla**	ticket office
tarde	late
la **tarde**	afternoon, evening
por la **tarde**	in the afternoon, evening
la **tarea**	task
las **tareas domésticas**	domestic chores
la **tarifa**	tariff, price list
la **tarjeta**	postcard
el **tarro**	jar
la **tarta**	cake, tart
el **taxi**	taxi
la **taza**	cup
te	(to) me
el **té**	tea
el **teatro**	drama
el **tebeo**	comic book
el **techo**	roof
la **tecla**	key
el **teclado**	keyboard
la **técnica**	technique
la **tecnología**	technology
el **tejado**	roof
la **tela**	fabric
la **telaraña**	spider diagram

A B C D E F G H I J K L M N O P Q R S **T** U V W X Y Z

la tele	television
telefonear	to telephone
el teléfono	telephone
el teléfono manos libres	hands-free phone
la telenovela	soap opera
la televisión	television
el tema	theme, subject
la temperatura	temperature
el templo	temple
temprano	early
la tendera	shopkeeper (female)
el tendero	shopkeeper (male)
tenemos	we have
tener	to have, to hold
tener ganas	to feel like it
Tenerife	Tenerife
tener que	to have to
tengo ... años	I'm ... (years old)
tengo calor	I'm hot
tengo hambre	I'm hungry
tengo sed	I'm thirsty
tengo (un/una) ...	I've got (a) ...
no tengo (un/una) ...	I haven't got (a) ...
el tenis	tennis
el tenista	tennis player (male)
la tenista	tennis player (female)
la tensión	stress
la tercera	the third
tercero	third
termina	it finishes
terminan	they finish
terminar	to finish
la terraza	terrace
terrible	terrible
el terror	horror
el tesoro	treasure
el test	test
el texto	text
ti	(to) you
la tía	aunt
el tiburón	shark
el tiempo	time, weather
hace buen tiempo	the weather's fine
mucho tiempo	a long time
¿qué tiempo hace?	what's the weather like?
el tiempo libre	free time

■ = masculine noun ■ = feminine noun ■ = verb ■ = adjectiv

la	**tienda**	shop
la	**tienda de camping**	tent
la	**tienda de periódicos**	newsagent's
la	**tienda de regalos**	gift shop
	tiene ... años ...	is ... (years old)
	tienes	you have (got) (*tú*, informal)
	¿tienes hermanos?	have you got any brothers and sisters?
	¿tienes un/una ...?	have you got a …?
la	**tierra**	earth, land, ground
las	**tijeras**	scissors
	tímido	shy, timid
el	**tío**	uncle/aunt
	típico	typical
el	**tipo**	type, kind, sort
	tirar	to throw, to pull
la	**tirita**	plaster (for cut)
el	**título**	title
los	**títulos**	qualifications
la	**toalla**	towel
el	**tobillo**	ankle
te	**toca**	it's your turn
el	**tocador**	dressing table
	tocar	to touch, to play (an instrument)
	tocar la guitarra/el piano	to play the guitar/piano
	toco la guitarra/el piano	I play the guitar/piano
en	**todas partes**	everywhere
	todavía	still, yet
	todo	all, every
	todo el mundo	everybody, everyone
	todo recto	straight on
	todos	all
	todos los días	every day
	toma/tome	here you are/take it
	tomar	to take
	tomar el sol	to sunbathe
	tomas	you have (to drink or eat) (*tú*, informal)
el	**tomate**	tomato
	tonto	silly, stupid
el	**top**	top (clothes)
	torcer	to turn
el	**torero**	bullfighter
la	**tormenta**	storm
el	**torneo**	tournament
el	**toro**	bull
	torpe	clumsy

A B C D E F G H I J K L M N O P Q R S **T** U V W X Y Z

la **torre**	tower
la **tortilla**	omelette
la **tortilla española**	Spanish omelette (made with onions and potatoes)
la **tortuga**	tortoise
la **tos**	cough
la **tostada**	slice of toast
en **total**	in total
totalmente	totally
trabajador(a)	hardworking
trabajar	to work
el **trabajo**	work
los **trabajos manuales**	handicrafts
la **tradición**	tradition
tradicional	traditional
traducir	to translate
me **traéis**	bring me (*vosotros* command)
traer	to bring
el **tráfico**	traffic
el **traje**	costume, suit
tranquilo	peaceful, quiet, calm, still
el **transbordador espacial**	space shuttle
el **tratamiento**	treatment
tratar (de)	to try (to)
tratar(se) de	to be about
travieso	naughty
el **tren**	train
en **tren**	by train
tres	three
el **trigo**	wheat
triste	sad
el **trozo**	piece, slice
la **trucha**	trout
tu	your (singular)
tú	you
el **tubo**	tube
tuerce	turn (*tú* command)
el **túnel**	tunnel
el **turismo**	tourism
el **turista**	tourist (male)
la **turista**	tourist (female)
el **turrón**	nougat
tus	your (plural)
la **tutoría**	study period
tuyo	yours

■ = masculine noun ■ = feminine noun ■ = verb ■ = adjectiv

Uu

	u	or (before *o* and *ho*)
	Ud. (usted)	you (formal)
	último	last
	un/uno/una	a, one
la	**uña**	nail
	unas	some
	único	only
	unido	united
el	**uniforme**	uniform
la	**Unión Europea**	European Union
	unir	to join, link
la	**universidad**	university
	uno	one
	unos	some
	urbano	urban
la	**urgencia**	emergency
	Uruguay	Uruguay
	uruguayo	Uruguayan
	usar	to use
	usted	you (formal)
	útil	useful
	utilizar	to use
la	**uva**	grape

A B C D E F G H I J K L M N O P Q R S T U **V** W X Y Z

Vv

	va	he/she/it is going, you are going (*usted*, formal)
la	vaca	cow
de	vacaciones	on holiday
las	vacaciones	holidays
	vacío	empty
	vago	lazybones
	vainilla	vanilla
	vale	OK
	valer	to be worth
el	valle	valley
	¡vamos!	come on!, let's go!
	vamos ...	we're going ...
	van	they are going
	van a ...	they're going to ...
los	vaqueros	jeans
	varios	several
	vasco	Basque
el	vaso	glass (for drinking)
el	vaso de leche	glass of milk
	Vd. (usted)	you (formal)
a	veces	sometimes
muchas	veces	often
la	vecina	neighbour (female)
el	vecino	neighbour (male)
	vegetariano	vegetarian
el	vehículo	vehicle
	veinte	twenty
la	vela	sailing
	ve la tele	he/she watches TV
la	velocidad	speed
	vende	it sells
	vender	to sell
	venezolano	Venezuelan
	Venezuela	Venezuela
	venir	to come
la	ventaja	advantage
la	ventana	window
	veo la tele	I watch TV
	ver	to see, to watch
el	verano	summer
	verás	you will see (*tú*, informal)

■ = masculine noun ■ = feminine noun ■ = verb ■ = adjectiv

la	**verbena**	open-air dance
el	**verbo**	verb
la	**verdad**	truth
	verdadero	true
	verde	green
la	**verdulería**	greengrocer's
las	**verduras**	vegetables
	ver la tele(visión)	to watch TV
	verter	to pour
el	**vestido**	dress
	vestir(se)	to dress (to get dressed)
la	**veterinaria**	vet (female)
el	**veterinario**	vet (male)
una	**vez**	once
la	**vez (las veces)**	time
	vi	I saw
	viajamos	we travel(led)
	viajar	to travel
el	**viaje**	journey, trip
la	**viajera**	traveller (female)
el	**viajero**	traveller (male)
la	**vida**	life
el	**vídeo**	video
la	**vídeoconsola**	video game console
el	**videojuego**	video/computer game
la	**vieja**	old person (female)
el	**viejo**	old person (male)
el	**viento**	wind
hace	**viento**	it's windy
(el)	**viernes**	(on) Friday
el	**VIH**	HIV
el	**villancico**	Christmas carol
el	**vino**	wine
	violeta	violet
la	**visita**	visit
	visitar	to visit
la	**vista**	view
la	**vista al mar**	seaview
te	**vistes**	you get dressed (*tú*, informal)
la	**vitamina**	vitamin
	viven en ...	they live in ..., you live in ... (*ustedes*, formal)
	vivir	to live
	vivo (en) ...	I live (in) ...
la	**Vizcaya**	Biscay (Spanish province)

= masculine noun = feminine noun = verb = adjective

A B C D E F G H I J K L M N O P Q R S T U V W X Y Z

el	vocabulario	vocabulary
	volar	to fly
el	volcán	volcano
el	voleibol	volleyball
	volver	to return, to go back
	vomitar	to be sick
	vosotros/vosotras	you (plural)
	voy	I'm going
	voy a acostarme a las ...	I'm going to go to bed at ... o'clock
	voy al campo	I go to the country
	voy al cine	I go to the cinema
	voy al instituto	I go to school
	voy de compras	I go shopping
la	voz	voice
(en)	voz alta	aloud, out loud
la	vuelta	return
	vuestro/a	your (plural)

■ = masculine noun ■ = feminine noun ■ = verb ■ = adjectiv

Yy

	y	and
	ya	now, already
	yo	I
el	**yogur**	yoghurt

A B C D E F G H I J K L M N O P Q R S T U V W X **Y** Z

Zz

la	**zanahoria**	carrot
la	**zapatería**	shoe shop
las	**zapatillas**	trainers, slippers
las	**zapatillas de deporte**	sports shoes, trainers
las	**zapatillas deportivas**	trainers
el	**zapato**	shoe
la	**zarzuela**	Spanish operetta
el	**zoo**	zoo
la	**zoóloga**	zoologist (female)
el	**zoólogo**	zoologist (male)
la	**zorra**	fox
los	**zuecos**	clogs
el	**zumo**	juice
el	**zumo de naranja**	orange juice

■ = masculine noun ■ = feminine noun ■ = verb ■ = adjectiv

English – Spanish

Aa

to be	able	poder
	about	sobre
	above, on	encima de
	abroad	el extranjero
	active	activo
	activity	la actividad
	actor	el actor
	actress	la actriz
	address	la dirección
	advantage	la ventaja
	adventure	la aventura
	advertisement	el anuncio
	advice	el consejo
	aeroplane	el avión
to be	afraid	tener miedo
	after	después de
	afternoon	la tarde
in the	afternoon	por la tarde
	afternoon snack	la merienda
	afterwards, then	después
	Africa	Africa
	African	africano
	again	otra vez
	against	contra
	age	la edad
I	agree	estoy de acuerdo
	AIDS	el SIDA
	air	el aire
	airport	el aeropuerto
	alarm clock	el despertador
	all, every	todo
	all, everything	todo
	alone	solo
	alright	está bien
	alright, so-so	regular
	also	también
	always	siempre
	a.m.	de la mañana
I	am	soy, estoy
I	am ... (years old)	tengo ... años
	America	América, los Estados Unidos

= masculine noun = feminine noun = verb = adjective

A B C D E F G H I J K L M N O P Q R S T U V W X Y Z

A
B
C
D
E
F
G
H
I
J
K
L
M
N
O
P
Q
R
S
T
U
V
W
X
Y
Z

	American	estadounidense
I	**am from ...**	soy de ...
	amongst	entre
	and	y (e *before* i *and* hi)
	angry	enfadado
	animal	el animal
	ankle	el tobillo
	answer	la respuesta
to	**answer**	responder
	antiseptic	antiséptico
	apple	la manzana
	April	abril
you	**are (*tú*, informal)**	eres, estás
you	**are (*usted*, formal)**	es, está
they	**are**	son, están
	area, zone	la zona
	are you ...? (*tú*, informal)	¿eres ...?, ¿estás ...?
	Argentina	Argentina
	Argentinian	argentino
	arm	el brazo
	armchair	la butaca, el sillón
to	**arrive**	llegar
I	**arrive (home/at school)**	llego (a casa/al instituto)
he/she	**arrives home**	llega a casa
	art	el arte, el dibujo
	artistic	artístico
to	**ask**	preguntar
	aspirin	la aspirina
	at	en, a
	athletics	el atletismo
	attic	el desván
	August	agosto
	aunt	la tía
	Australia	Australia
	Australian	australiano
	Austria	Austria
	Austrian	austríaco
	autumn	el otoño
	avenue	la avenida, el paseo

■ = masculine noun ■ = feminine noun ■ = verb ■ = adjectiv

A B C D E F G H I J K L M N O P Q R S T U V W X Y Z

Bb

	baby	el bebé
to do	**babysitting**	trabajar de canguro
	back	la espalda
	bad	mal
	badminton	el bádminton
it's	**bad weather**	hace mal tiempo
school	**bag**	la mochila
sleeping	**bag**	el saco de dormir
	bagpipes	las gaitas
	baker's	la panadería
	Balearic Islands	Islas Baleares
	ball	la pelota
	ballpoint pen	el bolígrafo
	banana	el plátano
	bank	el banco
	bar	el bar
	barbecue	la barbacoa
	basement	el sótano
	basin	el lavabo
	basketball	el baloncesto
	bath	el baño
to have a	**bath**	bañarse
	bathroom	el baño, el cuarto de baño
to	**be**	ser, estar
to	**be able**	poder
	beach	la playa
	beans	las judías
	beard	la barba
	beautiful	guapo
	because	porque
	bed	la cama
to go to	**bed**	acostarse
	bedroom	el dormitorio
	bedside table	la mesilla, la mesita
	beef	la carne de vaca
	beer	la cerveza
	before	antes (de)
to	**begin**	empezar
	behind	detrás (de), atrás
to	**believe**	creer
	bell	la campana
	below	debajo (de)

belt	el cinturón
beside	al lado (de)
best	el/la mejor
between	entre
bicycle	la bicicleta
big	grande
by bike	en bicicleta
bin	la papelera
biology	la biología
bird	el pájaro
biro	el bolígrafo
birthday	el cumpleaños
happy birthday!	¡feliz cumpleaños!
biscuit	la galleta
black	negro
blackboard	la pizarra
blind	ciego
blinds	las persianas
block of flats	el bloque
blond	rubio
blouse	la blusa
blue	azul
boat	el barco
body	el cuerpo
bone	el hueso
book	el libro
bookcase	la librería
bookshop	la librería
boot	la bota
bored, boring	aburrido
bottle	la botella
bottom	el fondo
at the bottom (of)	al fondo (de)
bowling alley	la bolera
box	la caja
boy	el chico, el niño
boyfriend	el novio
boys and girls	los chicos
boys' school	el instituto masculino
bracelet	la pulsera
brand, make	la marca
Brazil	Brasil
Brazilian	brasileño
bread	el pan
break, playtime	el recreo

■ = masculine noun ■ = feminine noun ■ = verb ■ = adjectiv

	breakfast	el desayuno
to have	**breakfast**	desayunar
you have	**breakfast (*tú*, informal)**	desayunas
to	**breathe**	respirar
	bridge	el puente
to	**bring**	traer
	brother	el hermano
	brothers (and sisters)	los hermanos
	brown	castaño, marrón/marrones
to	**brush one's hair**	peinarse
to	**brush one's teeth**	lavarse los dientes
to	**build**	edificar
	building	el edificio
	bull	el toro
	bullfight	la corrida, la lidia
	bullfighter	el torero
	bus	el autobús
by	**bus**	en autobús
	bus station	la estación de autobuses
	bus stop	la parada de autobús
	busy	ocupado
	but	pero
	butcher's	la carnicería
	butter	la mantequilla
to	**buy**	comprar
	bye	hasta luego, adiós

A B C D E F G H I J K L M N O P Q R S T U V W X Y Z

Cc

	café	el café, la cafetería
	cake	el pastel
	calculator	la calculadora
	calendar	el calendario
to	**call**	llamar
to be	**called**	llamarse
	camera	la máquina (fotográfica)
	camping	el cámping
	campsite	el campamento
I	**can**	puedo
	Canary Islands	Islas Canarias
	canteen	la cantina
	cap	la gorra, el gorro
	capital (city)	la capital
	car	el coche
by	**car**	en coche
	cards (playing)	las cartas
be	**careful!**	¡cuidado!
	carnival	el carnaval
	car park	el aparcamiento
fitted	**carpet**	la moqueta
	carrot	la zanahoria
to	**carry**	llevar
	cartoon	los dibujos animados
	castanets	las catañuelas
	castle	el castillo
	cat	el gato
	cathedral	la catedral
	Catholic	católico
	CD	el disco compacto, el CD
to	**celebrate**	celebrar
(town)	**centre**	el centro (de la ciudad)
	cereal	los cereales
	chair	la silla
English	**Channel**	la Mancha
TV	**channel**	el canal
to	**chat**	charlar
to	**chat up**	ligar
	cheap	barato
	cheese	el queso
	chemistry	la química
	chemist's	la farmacia
	cherry	la cereza

■ = masculine noun ■ = feminine noun ■ = verb ■ = adjective

	chess	el ajedrez
	chest of drawers	la cómoda
	chicken	el pollo
	chickpeas	los garbanzos
	child	el niño/la niña
	childish	infantil
	Chile	Chile
it's	**chilly**	hace fresco
	chimney	la chimenea
	chips	las patatas fritas
	chocolate (drink/food)	el chocolate
(pork)	**chop**	la chuleta
	Christian	el cristiano/la cristiana
	Christianity	el crsitianismo
	Christmas	la Navidad
	Christmas Eve	la Nochebuena
	church	la iglesia
	cigarettes	los cigarillos
	cinema	el cine
	circle	el círculo
	city	la ciudad
	class, classroom	la clase
	clean	limpio
	clear	claro
I	**clear the table**	quito la mesa
to	**clear the table**	quitar la mesa
to	**click (on computer)**	pulsar
to	**climb**	escalar
	clock	el reloj
to	**close**	cerrar
	clothes, clothing	la ropa
	club	la discoteca
	coach (sport)	el entrenedor
	coach (transport)	el autocar
	coast	la costa
	coat	el abrigo
	cod	el bacalao
	coffee	el café
	cold	frío
I have a	**cold**	estoy resfriado, constipado
it's	**cold**	hace frío
to	**collect**	coleccionar
	collection	la colección
	college	el instituto
	Colombia	Colombia
	colour	el color

A B C D E F G H I J K L M N O P Q R S T U V W X Y Z

	comb	el peine
I	**comb my hair**	me peino
you	**comb your hair (*tú*, informal)**	te peinas
to	**come**	venir
	comfortable	cómodo
	compact disc	el disco compacto
pair of	**compasses**	el compás
to	**compete**	competir
	complaint	la queja
	computer	el ordenador
	computer game	el videojuego
	congratulations!	¡enhorabuena!
	contact lens	la lente de contacto
	continue (*tú* command)	sigue
	conversation	la conversación
I	**cook**	cocino
to	**cook**	cocinar
	cooker	la cocina
	cooking	la cocina
it's	**cool**	hace fresco
to	**copy and paste**	copiar y pegar
to	**correspond (by letter)**	cartearse
	corridor	el pasillo
	Costa Rica	Costa Rica
	costume	el traje
	cosy	acogedor
	cotton	el algodón
	cough	la tos
	country	el país
(in) the	**country**	(en) el campo
	countryside	el campo
	cousin	el primo/la prima
	cream (food)	la nata
	cream (ointment)	la pomada
	crème caramel	el flan
	cricket	el críquet
	crisps	las patatas fritas
to get	**cross**	enfadarse
to	**cross**	cruzar
to	**cry**	llorar
	cup	la taza
	cupboard	el armario
	curly	rizado
	curtains	las cortinas
to	**cut**	cortar
	cycling	el ciclismo

■ = masculine noun ■ = feminine noun ■ = verb ■ = adjectiv

Dd

	dad	papá
	daily routine	la rutina diaria
to	**dance**	bailar
	dancing	el baile
	dangerous	peligroso
	dark (colour)	oscuro
	dark (hair/skin)	moreno
	date	la fecha
	daughter	la hija
	day	el día
	dead	muerto
	deaf	sordo
	dear	querido
	December	diciembre
to	**decide**	decidir
to	**delete**	cancelar
	delicious	delicioso
	deodorant	el desodorante
	department store	las (grandes) almacenes
to	**describe**	describir
	description	la descripción
	desk	el escritorio, la mesa
	dessert	el postre
to	**destroy**	destruir
	destruction	la destrucción
	detail	el detalle
I	**detest**	detesto
	diary	la agenda
	dice	el dado
	dictionary	el diccionario
to	**die**	morir
	difference	la diferencia
	different	diferente
	difficult	difícil
	dining room	el comedor
	dinner/supper	la cena
I have	**dinner/supper**	ceno
to have	**dinner/supper**	cenar
	dirty	sucio
	disadvantage	la desventaja
	disaster	el desastre
	disco	la discoteca

A B C **D** E F G H I J K L M N O P Q R S T U V W X Y Z

to	discuss	discutir
	dish	el plato
	disk	el disco
	distance	la distancia
to	dive	bucear
	diver	el buzo
	DIY	el bricolaje
I	do	hago
to	do	hacer
	doctor	el médico/la médica
he/she	does	hace
he/she	does sport	hace deporte
	dog	el perro
	dolphin	el delfín
	Dominican	dominicano
the	Dominican Republic	la República Dominicana
	donkey	el burro
I	don't do anything	no hago nada
	door	la puerta
to	do sport	practicar el deporte
to	download	descargar
	downstairs	abajo
	dozen	una docena
	drama	el teatro
to	draw	dibujar
	drawing	el dibujo
	dream	el sueño
to	dream	soñar
	dress	el vestido
to	dress	vestirse
I get	dressed	me visto
	drink	la bebida
(soft)	drink	el refresco
to	drink	beber
to	drive	conducir
	driver	el conductor/la conductora
	driving licence	el carnet de conducir
	drug	la droga
	drum	el tambor
	during	durante
	DVD	el DVD

= masculine noun = feminine noun = verb = adjectiv

Ee

	English	Spanish
	each	cada
	ear	la oreja, el oído
	early	pronto, temprano
to	earn	ganar
	earring	el pendiente
	earth	la tierra
	easily	fácilmente
	east	el este
	Easter	la Pascua/la Semana Santa
	easy	fácil
I	eat	como
to	eat	comer
	Ecuador	Ecuador
	edge	el borde
	effort	el esfuerzo
	egg	el huevo
	eight	ocho
	eighteen	dieciocho
	eighth	octavo
	eighty	ochenta
	either	tampoco
	elbow	el codo
	electric guitar	la guitarra eléctrica
	electricity	la electricidad
	electronic	eléctronico
	elephant	el elefante
	eleven	once
	El Salvador	El Salvador
	e-mail	el correo electrónico
	emergency	la urgencia
	empty	vacío
	end (event)	el final
	end (film)	el fin
at the	end of	al final de
	energy	la energía
	engine	el motor
	England	Inglaterra
	English	inglés/inglesa
	English (language)	el inglés
	enjoyable	divertido
	enjoy your meal	¡que aproveche!
to	enjoy yourself	divertirse

A B C D E F G H I J K L M N O P Q R S T U V W X Y Z

A B C D **E** F G H I J K L M N O P Q R S T U V W X Y Z

	English	Spanish
	enough	bastante
	enthusiastic	aficionado
	entrance	la entrada
(at) the	**entrance**	(en) la entrada
	envelope	el sobre
	environment	el medio ambiente
	equals	son
	equipment	el equipo
	eraser	la goma
	especially	especialmente
	euro	el euro
	Europe	Europa
	European	europeo
	evening	la tarde
in the	**evening**	por la tarde
this	**evening**	esta tarde
	every	cada
	everybody	todo el mundo
	every day	todos los días
	everyone	todo el mundo
	everything	todo
	everywhere	en todas partes
	exam	el examen
	example	el ejemplo
for	**example**	por ejemplo
	excellent	excelente
	exchange	el intercambio
	exciting	emocionante
	excursion	la excursión
	exercise book	el cuaderno
	exercise (physical)	la gimnasia
	exercise (task)	el ejercicio
	exit	la salida
	expensive	caro
	experience	la experiencia
	experiment	el experimento
to	**explain**	explicar
	explanation	la explicación
to	**explore**	explorar
	explosion	la explosión
	eye	el ojo
	eyebrow	la ceja
	eyelash	la pestaña

■ = masculine noun ■ = feminine noun ■ = verb ■ = adjecti

Ff

	face	la cara
	factory	la fábrica
	fair/fair-haired	rubio
to	fall	caer
	false	falso
	family	la familia
	famous	famoso
	fan	el abanico
	fancy dress	el disfraz
	fantastic	fantástico
	far (from)	lejos (de)
	farm	la granja
	farmer	el agricultor/la agricultura
	fashion	la moda
	fashionable	de moda
not	fashionable	fuera de moda
	fast	rápido
	fast-food restaurant	el fast-food
	fat	gordo
	father	el padre
	favourite	favorito
	fear	el miedo
	February	febrero
I	feel	me siento
	felt-tip pen	el rotulador
	female	la hembra
	feminine	femenino
	festival	la fiesta
	field	el campo
	fifteen	quince
	fifth	quinto
	fifty	cincuenta
	fight	el combate/la lucha
to	fight	luchar
	file	la carpeta
	file (computer)	el fichero
	film	la película
	finally	finalmente
to	find	encontrar
to	find and replace	buscar y reemplazar
	fine	bien
	finger	el dedo

A B C D E F G H I J K L M N O P Q R S T U V W X Y Z

■ = masculine noun ■ = feminine noun ■ = verb ■ = adjective

they	**finish**	terminan
to	**finish**	terminar
it	**finishes**	termina
	fire	el fuego
	firefighter	el bombero
	fireworks	los fuegos artificiales
	first	primer/primero/primera
the	**first floor**	el primer piso, la primera planta
	first of all	primero
the	**first of (May)**	el primero/uno de (mayo)
	fish	el pez (los peces)
	fish (to eat)	el pescado
to	**fish**	pescar
	fisherman	el pescador
	fishing	la pesca
	fishing rod	la caña de pescar
	fishmonger's	la pescadería
	fit (sport)	en forma
	fitness	la salud
	five	cinco
	flag	la bandera
	flamenco (music, dance)	el flamenco
	flask	la cantimplora
	flat	el piso
	flat	llano
	floor	la planta
	floppy disk	el disquete
	flour	la harina
	flower	la flor
I have	**flu**	tengo la gripe
	flute	la flauta
	fly	la mosca
it's	**foggy**	hay niebla
	folder	la carpeta
to	**follow**	seguir
	following	siguiente
	food	la comida
	foot	el pie
on	**foot**	a pie
	football	el fútbol
	football match	el partido de fútbol
	football player	el futbolista/la futbolista
	for	para
	for example	por ejemplo
	for (time)	durante

	forty	cuarenta
	fountain	la fuente
	four	cuatro
	fourteen	catorce
	fourth	cuarto
	fox	la zorra
	France	Francia
	freckle	la peca
	free	libre
	free (no cost)	gratuito
	free time	el tiempo libre
to	**freeze**	helar
to	**freeze (food)**	congelar
	freezer	el congelador
	French	francés/francesa
	French (language)	el francés
	French stick	la barra de pan
	frequent	frecuente
	fresh, cool	fresco
(on)	**Friday**	(el) viernes
	fridge	la nevera, el frigorífico
	friend	el amigo/la amiga
	friendly	simpático
	frightened	asustado
	from	de/del/de la
	from, since	desde
in	**front of**	delante de
	fruit	la fruta
	fruit juice	el zumo de fruta
	fruit shop	la frutería
	Fuerteventura	Fuerteventura
	full	lleno
	fun	divertido
he/she has	**fun**	se divierte
I have	**fun**	me divierto
	funfair	la feria
	funny	divertido, genial
	furniture	los muebles
	future	el futuro

A B C D E F G H I J K L M N O P Q R S T U V W X Y Z

Gg

	game	el juego
	games room	la sala de juegos
	garage	el garaje
	garden	el jardín
	gardener	el jardinero
	garlic	el ajo
	gas	el gas
	gate	la puerta
shower/bath	gel	el gel de ducha
	generally	generalmente
	generous	generoso
	geography	la geografía
	German (language)	el alemán
	German (nationality)	alemán/alemana
	Germany	Alemania
to	get	obtener
to	get cross	enfadarse
to	get dressed	vestirse
to	get off (bus)	bajar de
to	get on with	llevarse bien con
he/she	gets up	se levanta
to	get undressed	quitarse los vestidos
I	get up	me levanto
I don't	get up	no me levanto
to	get up	levantarse
you	get up (*tú*, informal)	te levantas
	gift	el regalo
	ginger (hair)	rojo
	girl	la chica, la niña
	girlfriend	la novia
to	give	dar
	glass	el vaso
	glass (drinking)	la copa, el vaso
	glasses (spectacles)	las gafas
	glove	el guante
	glue	la cola
to	go	ir
	goal	el gol
I	go/am going (to)	voy (a)
they	go/are going	van
we	go/are going	vamos
to	go back	volver

■ = masculine noun ■ = feminine noun ■ = verb ■ = adjectiv

to	**go down**	bajar
	go down (*tú* command)	baja
he/she	**goes/is going**	va
he/she	**goes to bed**	se acuesta
to	**go in**	entrar
I am	**going to get up**	voy a levantarme
	gold	el oro
	golden	dorado
	goldfish	el pez de colores
	golf	el golf
	good	bueno
	good, well	bien
	good afternoon, evening	buenas tardes
	goodbye	adiós
	good idea	buena idea
	good luck	buena suerte
	good morning	buenos días
	goodnight	buenas noches
I	**go out**	salgo
to	**go out**	salir
I	**go shopping**	voy de compras
to	**go shopping**	ir de compras
I've	**got**	tengo
I	**go to bed**	me acuesto
to	**go to bed**	acostarse
you	**go to bed (*tú*, informal)**	te acuestas
to	**go up**	subir
	go up (*tú* command)	sube
	grandfather	el abuelo
	grandmother	la abuela
	grandparents	los abuelos
	grapefruit	el pomelo
	grapes	las uvas
	grass	la hierba
	greasy	grasiento
	great!	¡fenomenal!, ¡genial!
	Great Britain	Gran Bretaña
	great-grandfather	el bisabuelo
	great-grandmother	la bisabuela
	Greece	la Grecia
	green	verde
	grey	gris
	ground	la tierra, el suelo
	ground floor	la planta baja
	group	el grupo

A B C D E F **G** H I J K L M N O P Q R S T U V W X Y Z

group of friends	la pandilla
to grow	crecer
Guatemala	Guatemala
Guatemalan	guatemalteco
to guess	adivinar
guest	el invitado/la invitada
guinea pig	el cobayo, el conejillo de Indias
guitar	la guitarra
gymnasium	el gimnasio
gymnastics	la gimnasia

■ = masculine noun ■ = feminine noun ■ = verb ■ = adjectiv

Hh

	hair	el pelo
	hairbrush	el cepillo para el pelo
	hairdresser	el peluquero, la peluquera
	hairdresser's	la peluquería
	hake	la merluza
	half	medio
it's	**half past ...**	son las ... y media
	hall	el salón de actos
	hallway	la entrada, el pasillo
	ham	el jamón
	hamburger	la hamburguesa
	hamster	el hámster
	hand	la mano
	handbag	el bolso
	handicrafts	los trabajos manuales
	handkerchief	el pañuelo
	hands-free phone	el teléfono manos libres
	handsome	guapo
to	**hang around**	frecuentar
to	**happen**	pasar
	happiness	la felicidad
	happy	contento, feliz
	happy birthday!	¡feliz cumpleaños!
	harbour	el puerto
	hard	duro
he/she	**has (got)**	tiene
	hat	la gorra, el gorro
I	**hate**	odio
I	**have**	tengo
to	**have**	tener
we	**have**	tenemos
to	**have a cold**	estar resfriado, constipado
to	**have fun**	divertirse
you	**have (got) (*tú*, informal)**	tienes
I	**haven't got**	no tengo
to	**have to**	tener que
	have you got any brothers and sisters?	¿tienes hermanos?
	he	él
	head	la cabeza
	headache	el dolor de cabeza
	headphones	los auriculares

A B C D E F G H I J K L M N O P Q R S T U V W X Y Z

	health	la salud
	healthy	sano
to	**hear**	oír
	heart	el corazón
	heat	el calor
	heavy	pesado
	heel	el tacón
	height	la altura
	hello	hola
	helmet	el casco
I	**help**	ayudo
to	**help**	ayudar
you	**help (*tú*, informal)**	ayudas
	her	ella, su/sus
	here	aquí
	here is/are	hay
	hers	suyo
	hi!	¡hola!
	high	alto
	hill	la colina
	him	él
to	**hire**	alquilar
	his	suyo
	his	su/sus
	historic	histórico
	history	la historia
	hit	el golpe
to	**hit**	golpear
	HIV	el VIH
	hobby	el pasatiempo
	hockey	el hockey
to	**hold**	tener
on	**holiday**	de vacaciones
	holidays	las vacaciones
	home	la casa
	homeless	sin hogar
	homework	los deberes
	Honduran	hondureño
	Honduras	Honduras
	honey	la miel
	hood	la capucha
I	**hoover**	paso la aspiradora
to	**hoover**	pasar la aspiradora
to	**hope**	esperar
	horror film	la película de terror

■ = masculine noun ■ = feminine noun ■ = verb ■ = adjective

	horse	el caballo
	horse riding	la equitación
to go	**horse riding**	montar a caballo
	hospital	el hospital
	hot	caliente
I'm	**hot**	tengo calor
it's	**hot**	hace calor
	hot dog	el perrito caliente
	hour	una hora
	house	la casa, el chalet
	housework	los quehaceres domésticos, las tareas de la casa
	how?	¿cómo?
	how are things?	¿qué tal?
	how are you? (*tú*, informal)	¿cómo estás?
	how are you? (*usted*, formal)	¿cómo está usted?
	how do you come/ get to school? (*tú*, informal)	¿cómo llegas al instituto?
	how do you say… in Spanish?	¿cómo se dice…en español?
	how do you spell it?	¿cómo se escribe?
	however	sin embargo
	how far is it…?	¿cuánto hay…?
	how long…?	¿cuánto tiempo…?
	how many?	¿cuántos/as?
	how much is it?	¿cuánto es?
	how old are you? (*tú*, informal)	¿cuántos años tienes?
	hug	un abrazo
	huge	enorme
to be	**hungry**	tener hambre
to	**hurt**	doler
(one)	**hundred**	cien(to)
to	**hunt**	cazar
	hunting	la caza
to be in a	**hurry**	tener prisa
	husband	el marido

A B C D E F G H I J K L M N O P Q R S T U V W X Y Z

Ii

	I	yo
	I am	soy, estoy
	I am 12 years old	tengo doce años
	Ibiza	Ibiza
	ice cream	el helado
	ice rink	la pista de hielo
	ice skate	el patín de hielo
to go	**ice skating**	patinar sobre hielo
	ICT	la informática
	idea	la idea
	identification	la identificación
to	**identify**	identificar
	if	si
	ill	enfermo
	illness	la enfermedad
	image	la imagen
	imagination	la imaginación
to	**imagine**	imaginar
	immediately	inmediatamente
	important	importante
to	**improve**	mejorar
	in	en/durante
	in addition	además
	incredible	increíble
to	**indicate**	indicar
	industrial	industrial
	in fact	en realidad
	information	la información
	information technology	la informática
	ingredient	el ingrediente
	inhabitant	el habitante
	injury	la herida
	in my opinion	en mi opinión
	in particular	en particular
	insect	el insecto
	insect bite	la picadura
	instruction	la instrucción
	instrument	el instrumento
	intelligent	inteligente
	interesting	interesante
	international	internacional
	Internet	el Internet

■ = masculine noun ■ = feminine noun ■ = verb ■ = adjective

	Internet café	el café de Internet
	interview	la entrevista
	invitation	la invitación
to	**invite**	invitar
	Ireland	Irlanda
	Irish	irlandés/irlandesa
I	**iron**	plancho
to do the	**ironing, to iron**	planchar
he/she/it	**is**	es, está
	is/are there...?	hay...?
	island	la isla
he/she/it	**is...(years old)**	tiene...años
	Italian	italiano
	Italian (language)	el italiano
	Italian person	el italiano/la italiana
	Italy	Italia
	its	su
	it's four o'clock	son las cuatro

A B C D E F G H **I** J K L M N O P Q R S T U V W X Y Z

A B C D E F G H I J K L M N O P Q R S T U V W X Y Z

Jj

	jacket	la chaqueta
	jam	la mermelada
	Jamaica	Jamaica
	jamaican	jamaicano
	January	enero
	jar	el tarro, la jarra
	jealous	celoso
	jeans	los (pantalones) vaqueros
	Jew	el judío/la judía
	jewel	la joya
	Jewish	judío
	job	el trabajo
to go	**jogging**	hacer footing
to	**join**	unir
	joke	la broma
	journey	el viaje
(orange)	**juice**	el zumo (de naranja)
	July	julio
	jump	el salto
to	**jump**	saltar
	jumper	el jersey
	June	junio

■ = masculine noun ■ = feminine noun ■ = verb ■ = adjectiv

Kk

	keen	aficionado
to	**keep**	guardar
to	**keep fit**	mantenerse en forma
	key	la llave
	keyboard	el teclado
	keyring	el llavero
to	**kill**	matar
	kilo	el kilo
	kilometre	el kilómetro
	kind	amable
a	**kind, sort**	el tipo
	king	el rey
	kiss	el beso
to	**kiss**	besar
	kitchen	la cocina
	knee	la rodilla
	knickers	la braga
	knife	el cuchillo
to	**knock**	golpear
I don't	**know**	no sé
to	**know**	saber
to	**know (a person)**	conocer
(well)	**known**	(muy) conocido

■ = masculine noun ■ = feminine noun ■ = verb ■ = adjective

A B C D E F G H I J K **L** M N O P Q R S T U V W X Y Z

Ll

	label	la etiqueta
	lab(oratory)	el laboratorio
	lady	la señora
	lake	el lago
	lamb	el cordero
	lamp	la lámpara
	land	la tierra
	landscape	el paisaje
	language	el idioma, la lengua, el lenguaje
	language lab(oratory)	el laboratorio de idiomas
	Lanzarote	Lanzarote
	laptop	el ordenador portátil
	last	pasado
to	**last**	durar
	late	tarde
	later	más tarde
	law	la ley
I	**lay the table**	pongo la mesa
to	**lay the table**	poner la mesa
	lazy	perezoso
to	**learn**	aprender
to	**leave, go out**	salir
to the	**left (of)**	a la izquierda (de)
	leg	la pierna
	leisure centre	el polideportivo
	lemon	el limón
	lemonade	la limonada
to	**lend**	prestar
	length	el largo
	lentils	las lentejas
	less	menos
	lesson	la clase
	letter	la carta
	lettuce	la lechuga
	level	el nivel
	library	la biblioteca
	lid	la tapa
	life	la vida
	lift	el ascensor
to	**lift**	levantar
	light (colour)	claro
	light (weight)	ligero

■ = masculine noun ■ = feminine noun ■ = verb ■ = adjectiv

do you	**like …? (*tú*, informal)**	¿te gusta(n) …?
I	**like …**	me gusta(n) …
I don't	**like …**	no me gusta(n) …
I would	**like**	quiero, me gustaría
to	**like**	gustar
	line	la línea
	lip	el labio
	list	la lista
to	**listen to**	escuchar
	litre	el litro
	little	poco
a	**little**	un poco
I	**live**	vivo
to	**live**	vivir
	living room	el salón
	loft	el desván
to	**log off**	salir del sistema
to	**log on**	entrar al sistema
	London	Londres
	lonely	solo
	long	largo
a	**long time**	mucho tiempo
to	**look at**	mirar
to	**look for**	buscar
to	**look like**	parecerse
	lorry	el camión
to	**lose**	perder
	lost property	los objetos perdidos
	lots of	mucho
	lottery	la lotería
	loud	fuerte
	lounge-diner	el salón comedor
I	**love …**	me encanta …
lots of	**love**	abrazos
	love from (in a letter)	un abrazo
I	**love you**	te quiero
	low	bajo
to	**lower**	bajar
	luck	la suerte
good	**luck!**	¡qué tengas suerte!
	lunch	la comida
I have	**lunch**	como
	lunchtime	la hora de comer

A B C D E F G H I J K **L** M N O P Q R S T U V W X Y Z

Mm

	mad	loco
	magazine	la revista
	magic	el mágico
	magnificent	magnífico
	main square	la plaza mayor
	Majorca	Mallorca
to	**make/do**	hacer
to	**make a mistake**	equivocarse
he/she	**makes the bed**	hace la cama
	make-up	el maquillaje
	male	el macho
	man	el hombre
	many	mucho
how	**many?**	¿cuántos?
	map	el mapa
	March	marzo
to	**mark**	marcar
	market	el mercado
	marmalade	la mermelada
	marriage	el matrimonio
	married	casado
to	**marry**	casar
	masculine	masculino
	mass	la misa
	match	la cerilla
	match (sport)	el partido
	maths	las matemáticas
it doesn't	**matter**	no importa
what's the	**matter?**	¿qué te pasa?
	mattress	el colchón
	May	mayo
	maybe	quizá(s)
	mayor	el alcalde
	mayoress	la alcaldesa
(to)	**me**	me
	meal	la comida
to	**measure**	medir
	meat	la carne
	mechanic	el mecánico/la mecánica
	medicine	la medicina
	Mediterranean	mediterráneo
	medium height/size	de talla mediana

■ = masculine noun ■ = feminine noun ■ = verb ■ = adjectiv

to meet	encontrar(se)
we meet	nos encontramos
member	el miembro
me neither	yo tampoco
to mention	mencionar
menu	la carta
message	el mensaje
metal	el metal
me too	yo también
metre	el metro
Mexico	Méjico, México
midnight	la medianoche
midnight mass	la misa del gallo
military service	la mili
milk	la leche
milkshake	el batido
mine	mío
mineral water	el agua mineral
Minorca	Menorca
mirror	el espejo
mixed school	el instituto mixto
mobile phone	el móvil
model	el modelo
modern	moderno
moment	el momento
at the moment	de momento
(on) Monday	(el) lunes
monitor (TV, computer)	el monitor
moon	la luna
money	el dinero
monkey	el mono
month	el mes
monument	el monumento
more	más
morning	la mañana
in the morning	por la mañana
this morning	esta mañana
mosque	la mezquita
most	más
mother	la madre
motorbike	la moto
by motorbike	en moto
motorway	la autopista
mountain	la montaña
mountain bike	la bicicleta de montaña

A B C D E F G H I J K L M N O P Q R S T U V W X Y Z

	mouse (animal, computer)	el ratón
	moustache	el bigote
	mouth	la boca
to	**move**	mover
to	**move house**	mudarse
	Mr	Señor
	Mrs	Señora
how	**much?**	¿cuánto/a?
not	**much**	poco
	museum	el museo
	music	la música
	musician	el músico/la música
I	**must**	debo
	mustard	la mostaza
	my	mi/mis
	mystery	el misterio

■ = masculine noun ■ = feminine noun ■ = verb ■ = adjecti

Nn

nail	la uña
name	el nombre
(sur) name	el apellido
his/her name is	se llama
my name is	me llamo
afternoon nap	la siesta
narrow	estrecho
national	nacional
nationality	la nacionalidad
national park	el parque nacional
nature	la naturaleza
nearby	por aquí
nearly	casi
near (to)	cerca (de)
necessary	necesario
neck	el cuello
necklace	el collar
I need	me hace falta, necesito
to need	necesitar
negative	negativo
neighbour	el vecino/la vecina
neighbourhood	el barrio
neither	tampoco
neither ... nor ...	ni ... ni ...
nest	el nido
the Netherlands	los Países Bajos
network	la red
never	nunca
new	nuevo
news	las noticias
newsagent's	la tienda de periódicos
newspaper	el periódico
New Year	el Año Nuevo
New Year's Eve	la Nochevieja
New Year's resolutions	los buenos propósitos de fin de año
New Zealand	Nueva Zelanda
from New Zealand	neozelandés/neozelandesa
next	próximo
next to	al lado (de)
Nicaragua	Nicaragua
Nicaraguan	nicaragüense
nice	simpático, majo

A B C D E F G H I J K L M N O P Q R S T U V W X Y Z

it's	**nice weather**	hace buen tiempo
	night	la noche
at	**night**	por la noche
	nine	nueve
	nineteen	diecinueve
	ninety	noventa
	ninth	noveno
	no	no
	nobody	nadie
	noise	el ruido
	noisy	ruidoso
	normal	normal
	normally	normalmente
	north	el norte
	Northern Ireland	Irlanda del Norte
to the	**north of**	al norte de
	nose	la nariz
	note	la nota
	nothing	nada
	nothing else	nada más
	notice	el aviso
	November	noviembre
	now	ahora
	number	el número
	nurse	el enfermero/la enfermera
	nutritious	nutritivo

Oo

	OAP	el pensionista/la pensionista
	object	el objeto
	objective	el objetivo
	obligatory	obligatorio
to	**obtain**	obtener
	obvious	obvio
	ocean	el océano
at one	**o'clock**	a la una
it's one	**o'clock**	es la una
	October	octubre
	of	de, del
	of course	desde luego
	office	el despacho
	official	oficial
	often	muchas veces, a menudo
	oil	el aceite
	OK	de acuerdo, está bien, vale
	old	antiguo
	older	mayor
	old-fashioned	pasado de moda
	olive	la aceituna
	omelette	la tortilla
Spanish	**omelette**	la tortilla española
	on	en, encima de, sobre
	on, about	sobre
	on, at	en
	once	una vez
	once again	otra vez
	one	un/uno/una
	on foot	a pie
	on holiday	de vacaciones
	onion	la cebolla
	only	sólo, solamente
	only child	el hijo único/la hija única
	on time	a la hora, puntual
	open	abierto
to	**open**	abrir
	opinion	la opinión
	opposite	enfrente (de)
	or	o (u *before* o *and* ho)
	orange (colour)	color naranja
	orange (fruit)	la naranja

A B C D E F G H I J K L M N **O** P Q R S T U V W X Y Z

■ = masculine noun ■ = feminine noun ■ = verb ■ = adjective

A B C D E F G H I J K L M N **O** P Q R S T U V W X Y Z

orangeade	la naranjada
orange juice	el zumo de naranja
order	el orden
to order (meal)	encargar
ordinary	corriente
organic	orgánico
organisation	la organización
to organise	organizar, arreglar
other	otro
(on) the outskirts	(en) las afueras
oven	el horno
over	sobre
owl	la lechuza
owner	el dueño/la dueña

= masculine noun = feminine noun = verb = adjectiv

Pp

	packet	el paquete
	paella	la paella
	page	la página
	pain	el dolor
to	**paint**	pintar
	painting	la pintura
	pair	el par
	pair of scissors	las tijeras
	Pakistan	Paquistán
	Pakistani	paquistaní
	palace	el palacio
	Palma	la Palma
	Panama	Panamá
	paper	el papel
	parade	la cabalgata, el desfile
	Paraguay	Paraguay
	parents	los padres
	park	el parque
to	**park**	aparcar
	parliament	el parlamento
	part	la parte
to	**participate**	participar
	partner	el compañero/la compañera
	party	la fiesta
to	**pass**	pasar
	passenger	el pasajero/la pasajera
	passport	el pasaporte
	password	la contraseña
	past	el pasado
	pasta	la pasta
	path	el camino
	patient	el paciente/la paciente
	pavement	la acera
to	**pay**	pagar
	PE	la educación física
	peaceful	tranquilo
	peanuts	los cacahuetes
	pear	la pera
	peas	los guisantes
to	**peel**	pelar
	pen (ballpoint)	el bolígrafo
	pen (felt-tip)	el rotulador

■ = masculine noun ■ = feminine noun ■ = verb ■ = adjective

A B C D E F G H I J K L M N O **P** Q R S T U V W X Y Z

	pen (fountain)	la pluma
	pencil	el lápiz, el lapicero
	pencil case	el estuche
	pencil sharpener	el sacapuntas
	penfriend	el amigo/la amiga por correspondencia
	penny	el penique
	people	la gente
	pepper (spice)	la pimienta
	pepper (sweet)	el pimiento
	perfect	perfecto
	perfume	el perfume
	perhaps	quizá(s)
	person	la persona
	Peru	Perú
	pet	el animal doméstico, la mascota
	petrol	la gasolina
	petrol station	la estación de servicio
	pharmacist	el farmacéutico/la farmacéutica
	pharmacy	la farmacia
	phone	el teléfono
to	**phone**	telefonear, llamar por teléfono
	photo	la foto
	photography	la fotografía
	physics	la física
	piano	el piano
to	**pick up**	recoger
	picnic	la merienda
	picture	el cuadro
	piece	el pedazo, el trozo
	pig	el cerdo
	pilot	el piloto
	pink	color de rosa
	pizza	la pizza
	place	el lugar
	plan	el plan
	plane	el avión
	planet	el planeta
	plant	la planta
to	**plant**	plantear
	plaster (for cut)	la tirita
	plastic	el plástico
	plate	el plato
I	**play**	juego
to	**play cards**	jugar a las cartas

■ = masculine noun ■ = feminine noun ■ = verb ■ = adjective

to play (game)	jugar
playground	el patio
playing cards	las cartas
to play (instrument)	tocar
to play on the computer	jugar con el ordenador
I play the guitar/piano	toco la guitarra/el piano
to play the guitar/piano	tocar la guitarra/el piano
to play video games	jugar con los videojuegos
to play with my PlayStation	jugar con mi PlayStation
please	por favor
plus	más
pocket	el bolsillo
pocket money	el dinero para gastos
poem	la poesía
pole (North/South)	el polo
police	la policía
policeman	el policía
policewoman	la policía
polite	cortés/cortesa
to pollute	contaminar
poor	pobre
pop music	la música pop
popular	popular
population	la población
pork	el cerdo
port	el puerto
portable	portátil
portion	la ración
Portugal	Portugal
Portuguese	portugués/portuguesa
posh	pijo
position	la posición
positive	positivo
possibility	la posibilidad
post	el correo
to post	echar al buzón, echar al correo
postage stamp	el sello
postcard	la postal
poster	el póster
postman	el cartero
post office	el correos
postwoman	la cartera
potato	la patata
pound (sterling)	la libra (esterlina)
to pour	verter

A B C D E F G H I J K L M N O **P** Q R S T U V W X Y Z

■ = masculine noun ■ = feminine noun ■ = verb ■ = adjective

A B C D E F G H I J K L M N O **P** Q R S T U V W X Y Z

	powerful	poderoso
	practical	práctico
to	practise	practicar
	prawn	la gamba
I	prefer	prefiero
to	prefer	preferir
	preparation	la preparación
to	prepare (supper)	preparar (la cena)
	prescription	la receta
	present	el regalo
	presentation	la exposición
	presenter	el presentador/la presentadora
	president	el presidente
to	press	apretar
	pretty	bonito
	previously	anteriormente
	price	el precio
	primary school	la escuela primaria
to	print	imprimir
	printer	la impresora
	prison	la cárcel
	private	privado
	problem	el problema
(street)	procession	el desfile
to	produce	producir
	product	el producto
	professional	profesional
	programme	el programa
	progress	el progreso
to	pronounce	pronunciar
to	protect	proteger
	protection	la protección
	protein	la proteína
	PSHE	la educación cívica
	public	el público
	pudding	el postre
to	pull	tirar
to	punish	castigar
	pupil	el alumno/la alumna
	purple	morado
	purse	el monedero
to	push	empujar
to	put	poner
to	put the rubbish out	sacar la basura
	pyjamas	el pijama

■ = masculine noun ■ = feminine noun ■ = verb ■ = adjective

Qq

	qualifications	los títulos
	quarter	el cuarto
it's	**quarter past ...**	son las ... y cuarto
it's	**quarter to ...**	son las ... menos cuarto
	queen	le reina
	question	la pregunta
	queue	la cola
	quick	rápido
	quiet	tranquilo
	quite	bastante

A B C D E F G H I J K L M N O P Q **R** S T U V W X Y Z

Rr

	rabbit	el conejo
	race	la carrera
	racism	el racismo
	racket (tennis)	la raqueta
	radiator	el radiador
	radio	el radio
	railway	el ferrocarril
	rain	la lluvia
to	**rain**	llover
it's	**raining**	llueve
	rat	la rata
	RE	la religión
to	**read**	leer
	ready	listo
to get	**ready**	prepararse
to	**realise**	darse cuenta de
	reason	el razón
	receipt	el recibo
to	**receive**	recibir
	recent	reciente
	recipe	la receta
to	**recommend**	recomendar
to	**record (computer)**	registrar
to	**record (music)**	grabar
to	**recycle**	reciclar
	recycling	el reciclaje
	red	rojo
	red-haired/red-headed	pelirrojo
to	**reduce**	reducir
	reduction	la reducción
to	**refund**	devolver
	region	la región
	register	la lista
	regularly	regularmente
	relationship	la relación
to	**relax**	descansar
	relaxing	relajante
	religion	la religión
	remote control	el telemando, el telecontrol
to	**rent**	alquilar
to	**repair**	reparar
to	**repeat**	repetir

■ = masculine noun ■ = feminine noun ■ = verb ■ = adjective

to reply	contestar
to report	informar
to rest	descansar
restaurant	el restaurante
result	el resultado
to return	volver
to revise	repasar
rice	el arroz
rich	rico
to ride	montar
I ride my bicycle	monto en bicicleta
right, correct	correcto
to the right (of)	a la derecha (de)
to risk	arriesgar
ring	el anillo
river	el río
road	la calle
rock	la roca
rollerblades	los patines en línea
rollerblading	el patinaje en línea
romantic	romántico
roof	el techo
room	la habitación
round	redondo
roundabout	la glorieta
routine	la rutina
row, line	la fila
rubber, eraser	la goma
rubbish	la basura
rucksack	la mochila
rug	la alfombra
rugby	el rugby
rule	la regla
ruler	la regla
to run	correr

A B C D E F G H I J K L M N O P Q R **S** T U V W X Y Z

Ss

	English	Spanish
	sad	triste
	safe	seguro
	saffron	el azafrán
	sailing	la vela
to go	**sailing**	salir en balandro
	sailing boat	el barco de vela
	salad	la ensalada
	salary	el sueldo
	sales	los saldos
	sales assistant	el dependiente/la dependienta
	salmon	el salmón
	salt	el sal
El	**Salvador**	El Salvador
	same	mismo
	sand	la arena
	sandal	la sandalia
	sandwich	el bocadillo
(on)	**Saturday**	(el) sábado
	sauce	la salsa
	sausage	la salchicha
to	**save**	salvar
to	**save (money)**	ahorrar
to	**say**	decir
	scarf	la bufanda
	school	el colegio
	school bag	la mochila
	school (primary)	la escuela
	school (secondary)	el instituto
	school subject	la asignatura
	science fiction	la ciencia-ficción
	science (subject)	las ciencias
	scientist	el científico/la científica
	scooter	el escúter
to	**score a goal**	marcar un gol
	Scotland	Escocia
	Scottish	escocés/escocesa
	screen	la pantalla
	sea	el mar
	seafood	los mariscos
	search engine	el buscador
	season	la estación
	sea view	la vista al mar

■ = masculine noun ■ = feminine noun ■ = verb ■ = adjectiv

	second	segundo
the	**second**	la segunda
	secondary school	el instituto
	second-hand	de segunda mano
	secret	secreto
	secretary	el secretario/la secretaria
to	**see**	ver
	see you later/soon	hasta luego
	selfish	egoísta
to	**sell**	vender
	semi-detached	adosado
to	**send**	enviar, mandar
to	**send text messages**	mandar mensajes
	sensitive	sensible
	sentence	la frase
to	**separate**	separar
	September	septiembre, setiembre
	series	la serie
	serious	serio
	settee	el sofá
	seven	siete
	seventeen	diecisiete
	seventh	séptimo
	seventy	setenta
	several	varios
	shampoo	el champú
	shape	la forma
to	**share**	compartir
to	**shave**	afeitarse
	sheep	la oveja
	shelf	la estantería
to	**shine**	brillar
	shirt	la camisa
	shoe	el zapato
	shoe shop	la zapatería
	shop	la tienda
to go	**shopping**	ir de compras
	shopping centre	el centro comercial
	short	bajo (*height*), corto (*hair*)
	shorts	el pantalón corto
to	**shout**	gritar
to	**show**	mostrar
	shower	la ducha
I have a	**shower**	me ducho
to have a	**shower**	ducharse

A B C D E F G H I J K L M N O P Q R **S** T U V W X Y Z

A B C D E F G H I J K L M N O P Q R S T U V W X Y Z

	showing	la sesión
to	**shut**	cerrar
	shy	tímido
	sick	enfermo
to be	**sick**	vomitar
to feel	**sick**	estar mareado
	silent	callado
	silly	tonto
	silver	la plata
	similar	parecido
	similarity	el parecido
	simple	sencillo
	simply	secillamente
	since	desde entonces
to	**sing**	cantar
	singer	el cantante/la cantante
	sink (kitchen)	el fregadero
	Sir	Señor
	sister	la hermana
to	**sit down**	sentarse
to be	**situated**	estar situado
	situation	la situación
	six	seis
	sixteen	dieciséis
	sixth	sexto
	sixty	sesenta
	size (clothes)	la talla
	size (shoes)	el número
to	**skate**	patinar
to go	**skateboarding**	andar/montar en monopatín
	skating	el patinaje
	skeleton	el esqueleto
to	**ski**	esquiar
	skiing	el esquí
	skin	la piel
	skirt	la falda
to	**sleep**	dormir
	sleeping bag	el saco de dormir
	sleeve	la manga
	slice	la porción
	slim	delgado
	slow	lento
	slowly	lentamente
	small	pequeño
	smart	elegante

■ = masculine noun ■ = feminine noun ■ = verb ■ = adjectiv

to **smell**	oler
to **smile**	sonreír
smoke	el humo
to **smoke**	fumar
afternoon **snack**	la merienda
snail	el caracol
snake	la serpiente
to **snore**	roncar
snow	la nieve
to **snow**	nevar
snowboard	el snowboard
it's **snowing**	nieva
soap	el jabón
soap opera	la telenovela
society	la sociedad
sock	el calcetín
sofa	el sofá
software	el software
soldier	el soldado/la soldado
solution	la solución
some	unos/unas
somebody	alguien
something	algo
sometimes	a veces
somewhere	en alguna parte
son	el hijo
song	la canción
soon	pronto
see you **soon**	hasta pronto
sore throat	el dolor de garganta
I am **sorry**	lo siento
sort	el tipo
to **sort out**	arreglar
so-so, alright	regular
sound system	el equipo de música
soup	la sopa
south	el sur
South America	Sudamérica
South American	sudamericano
souvenir	el recuerdo
space	el espacio
space shuttle	el transbordador espacial
space station	la estación espacial
spaghetti	los espaguetis
Spain	España

A B C D E F G H I J K L M N O P Q R **S** T U V W X Y Z

	Spanish	español(a)
	Spanish (language)	el español
	Spanish omelette	la tortilla española
I	**speak**	hablo
to	**speak**	hablar
	special	especial
	speed	la velocidad
to	**spell**	escribir
to	**spend (money)**	gastar
to	**spend (time)**	pasar
	spice	la especia
	spicy sausage	el chorizo
	spider	la araña
	spine	la columna vertebral
	spoon	la cucharra
	sport	el deporte
	sports centre	el polideportivo
	sportsman	el deportista
	sports pitch	la pista polideportiva
	sportswoman	la deportista
	sporty	deportivo
	spring	la primavera
(town)	**square**	la plaza
	square (shape)	el cuadrado
	squash	el squash
	squid	los calamares
	stadium	el estadio
	staffroom	la sala de profesores
	stairs	la escalera
	stamp	el sello
to	**stand up**	ponerse de pie
	star	la estrella
to	**start**	empezar
	starter	el entremés
	station	la estación
to	**stay**	quedarse, alojarse
	steak	el biftec
to	**steal**	robar
	step	el paso
	stepbrother	el hermanastro
	stepfather	el padrastro
	stepmother	la madrastra
	stepsister	la hermanastra
	stereo system	el estéreo
	stereotype	el estereotipo

■ = masculine noun ■ = feminine noun ■ = verb ■ = adjecti

	English	Spanish
	stew	el cocido
	stick	el palo
	sticker	la etiqueta
	still	todavía
	still (motionless)	inmóvil
	still (quiet)	tranquilo
to	**sting**	picar
to	**stir**	mover
	stomach	el estómago
to	**stop**	parar
	storey	la planta
	storm	la tormenta
it's	**stormy**	hay tormenta
	story	la historia
	straight	liso
	straight on	todo recto/derecho
	strange	estraño
	strawberry	la fresa
	street	la calle
	stress	la tensión
to	**stretch**	extender
	strict	severo
	striped	rayado
	strong	fuerte
	student	el estudiante/la estudiante
I	**study**	estudio
to	**study**	estudiar
	stupid	estúpido
	subject	la asignatura
	suburbs	las afueras
to	**succeed**	tener éxito
	success	el éxito
	suddenly	de repente
	sugar	el azúcar
to	**suggest**	sugerir
	suggestion	la sugerencia
	suit	el traje
	suitcase	la maleta
	summer	el verano
	summer camp	el campamento
	sun	el sol
to	**sunbathe**	tomar el sol
(on)	**Sunday**	(el) domingo
	sunglasses	las gafas de sol
it's	**sunny**	hace sol

A B C D E F G H I J K L M N O P Q R S T U V W X Y Z

A B C D E F G H I J K L M N O P Q R **S** T U V W X Y Z

	sunstroke	la insolación
	suntan	el bronceado
	suntan lotion	el bronceador
	super, great	estupendo
	supermarket	el supermercado
	supper	la cena
I have	**supper**	ceno
to have	**supper**	cenar
I go	**surfing**	hago surfing
to	**surf the Internet**	navegar por Internet
	surname	el apellido
	surprise	la sorpresa
	survey (poll)	la encuesta
	sweater	el jersey
	sweatshirt	la sudadera
to	**sweep**	barrer
	sweet	dulce
	sweets	los caramelos
to	**swim**	nadar
	swimming	la natación
	swimming costume/trunks	el bañador
	swimming pool	la piscina
	Swiss	suizo
to	**switch off (engine)**	parar
to	**switch off (light)**	apagar
to	**switch on**	encender
	Switzerland	la Suiza
	syrup	el jarabe
	system	el sistema

= masculine noun = feminine noun = verb = adjectiv

Tt

	tabby (cat)	atigrado
	table	la mesa
	table football	el futbolín
	tablet	la pastilla
	table tennis	el ping-pong, el tenis de mesa
	tail	la cola
to	**take**	tomar
to	**take care of**	cuidar
to	**take off (clothing)**	quitarse
to	**take off (plane)**	despegar
to	**take part in**	participar en
to	**take photos**	sacar fotos
to	**talk**	hablar
to	**talk on the telephone**	hablar por teléfono
	tall	alto
to get a	**tan**	ponerse moreno
	tape	la cinta
	tape recorder	el magnetofón
	task	la tarea
to	**taste**	probar
	taxi	el taxi
	tea	el té
	teacher	el profesor/la profesora
	team	el equipo
	technology	la tecnología
	teenager	el joven/la joven
(back)	**teeth**	los dientes (las muelas)
to brush one's	**teeth**	limpiar los dientes
	telephone	el teléfono
to	**telephone**	llamar por teléfono
	television	la televisión
to watch	**television**	ver la televisión
	television programme	el programa de televisión
to	**tell**	decir, llamar
	telly	le tele
	temperature	la temperatura
I have a	**temperature**	tengo fiebre
	temple	el templo
	ten	diez
	Tenerife	Tenerife
	tennis	el tenis

A B C D E F G H I J K L M N O P Q R S **T** U V W X Y Z

	tennis court	la pista de tenis
	tent	la tienda (de camping)
	tenth	décimo
	terrace	la terraza
	terrible	fatal
	test	la prueba
to	**text**	mandar un mensaje
	textbook	el libro (de texto)
	text message	el mensaje
to	**thank**	dar las gracias
	thanks to	gracias a
	thank you	gracias
	that	aquel(la)
	that	ese/esa
	that one	ése/ésa
	that's all	eso es todo
	that's it	ya está
	the	el, la, los, las
	theatre	el teatro
	their	su
	theme	el tema
	theme park	el parque temático
	then	después, luego
	there	allí
over	**there**	allá
	there is/are	hay
	these	estos/estas
	these ones	éstos/éstas
	they	ellos, ellas
	thick	espeso
	thin	delgado
	thing	la cosa
to	**think**	pensar
I	**think (that)**	pienso (que)
	third	tercero
I am	**thirsty**	tengo sed
to be	**thirsty**	tener sed
	this	este/esta
	this one	éste/ésta/esto
	those	aquellos
	those	esos/esas
	those ones	ésos/ésas
	thousand	mil
	threat	la amenaza
	three	tres

■ = masculine noun ■ = feminine noun ■ = verb ■ = adjectiv

	throat	la garganta
to	**throw**	tirar, lanzar
	thunderstorm	la tormenta
(on)	**Thursday**	(el) jueves
	ticket (bus/train)	el billete
	ticket (entrance)	la entrada
to	**tidy**	arreglar
	tie	la corbata
	tight-fitting	ajustado
	tights	las medias
on	**time**	a la hora, puntual
	time (clock)	la hora
	time (occasion)	la vez
	time (period)	el tiempo
	timetable	el horario
	tin	la lata
	tired	cansado
	title	el título
	to (the)	a la, al, a los, a las
	toast	el pan tostado, la tostada
	today	hoy
	together	junto
	toilet	el aseo
	toilets	los servicios
	tomato	el tomate
	tomorrow	mañana
	tongue	la lengua
	tonight	esta noche
	too	también
	tooth	el diente
	toothache	el dolor de muelas
	toothbrush	el cepillo de dientes
	toothpaste	la pasta de dientes
on	**top (of)**	encima (de)
	torch	la linterna
	tortoise	la tortuga
	total	en total
	totally	totalmente
to	**touch**	tocar
	tour	la excursión
	tourism	el turismo
	tourist	el turista/la turista
	tourist office	la oficina de turismo
	tournament	el torneo
	towards	hacia

A B C D E F G H I J K L M N O P Q R S **T** U V W X Y Z

	towel	la toalla
	town (city)	la ciudad
	town hall	el ayuntamiento
	town (small)	el pueblo
	toy	el juguete
	tracksuit	el chándal
	tradition	la tradición
	traffic	el tráfico
	traffic jam	el atasco
	traffic lights	el semáforo
	train	el tren
by	**train**	en tren
to	**train**	entrenar
	trainers	las zapatillas de deporte
	train station	la estación de trenes/de RENFE
to	**translate**	traducir
	transport	el transporte
to	**travel**	viajar
	traveller	el viajero/la viajera
	treasure	el tesoro
	treatment	el tratamiento
	tree	el árbol
	trendy	muy al día
	trip	el viaje, la excursión
	trousers	el pantalón
	true	verdadero
to	**try**	probar
	T-shirt	la camiseta
	tube	el tubo
(on)	**Tuesday**	(el) martes
	tunnel	el túnel
	turkey	el pavo
	turn (*tú* command)	dobla, tuerce
it's my	**turn**	me toca
to	**turn**	doblar, torcer
	TV	la televisión
	TV programme	el programa
	twelve	doce
	twenty	veinte
	twice	dos veces
	twins	los gemelos/las gemelas
	two	dos
	typical	típico

■ = masculine noun ■ = feminine noun ■ = verb ■ = adjectiv

Uu

	English	Spanish
	ugly	feo
	UK	el Reino Unido
	umbrella	el paraguas
	unbelievable	increíble
	uncle	el tío
	under	debajo (de)
by	**underground (train)**	en metro
to	**underline**	subrayar
	underneath	debajo (de)
	underpants	las calzonzillos
I don't	**understand**	no comprendo
to	**understand**	comprender
	underwear	la ropa interior
	unemployed	parado
	unemployment	el paro, el desempleo
	unfortunately	por desgracia, desgraciadamente
	unhappy	mal
	uniform	el uniforme
the	**United Kingdom**	el Reino Unido
the	**United States**	los Estados Unidos
	university	la universidad
	unpleasant	antipático
	untidy	desordenado
	until	hasta
	unwell	mal
	upstairs	arriba
	Uruguay	Uruguay
	Uruguayan	uruguayo
	us	nosotros
to	**use**	utilizar
I	**used to go**	iba
	useful	útil
	usually	generalmente, normalmente

■ = masculine noun ■ = feminine noun ■ = verb ■ = adjective

A B C D E F G H I J K L M N O P Q R S T U **V** W X Y Z

Vv

to	**vacuum**	pasar la aspiradora
	vacuum cleaner	la aspiradora
	van	la camioneta
	vanilla	la vainilla
	vase	el floreo
	vegetables	las verduras
	vegetarian	vegetariano
	vehicle	el vehículo
	Venezuela	Venezuela
	Venezuelan	venezolano
	verb	el verbo
	very	muy
I'm	**very well, thank you**	estoy muy bien gracias
	vet	el veterinario/la veterinaria
	video game	el videojuego
	video game console	el vídeoconsola
	view	la vista
	villa	el chalet
	village	el pueblo
	violet	violeta
	visit	la visita
to	**visit**	visitar
	visitor	el visitante/la visitante
	vitamin	la vitimina
	vocabulary	el vocabulario
	volleyball	el voleibol

■ = masculine noun ■ = feminine noun ■ = verb ■ = adjectiv

Ww

	waist	la cintura
to	**wait**	esperar
	waiter	el camarero
	waitress	la camerera
I	**wake up**	me despierto
to	**wake up**	despertarse
	Wales	Gales
	walk	el paseo
to	**walk**	andar
to	**walk the dog**	llevar al perro
I	**walk (to school)**	llego a pie
	wall	la pared
	wallet	el cartero
	want	querer
I	**want**	quiero
do you	**want to go out? (*tú*, informal)**	¿quieres salir?
	war	la guerra
	wardrobe	el armario
	war film	la película de guerra
	warm	caliente
to	**warn**	avisar
I	**was**	estaba, era
to	**wash**	lavar
	washbasin	el lavabo
	washing machine	la lavadora
to	**wash oneself**	lavarse
to	**wash the car**	lavar el coche
to	**wash the dishes**	fregar los platos
	watch	el reloj
to	**watch**	ver
to	**watch TV**	ver la tele(visión)
	water	el agua
	wave	la ola
	wavy	ondulado
	way of life	el estilo de vida
	we	nosotros/as
	weak	débil
I	**wear**	llevo
to	**wear**	llevar
	weather	el tiempo
	weather forecast	el pronóstico del tiempo
what's the	**weather like?**	¿qué tiempo hace?

A B C D E F G H I J K L M N O P Q R S T U V W X Y Z

	website	el sitio web
	wedding	la boda
(on)	**Wednesday**	(el) miércoles
	week	la semana
on	**weekdays**	durante la semana
(at) the	**weekend**	el fin de semana
to	**weigh**	pesar
	welcome	bienvenido
	well	bien
	well-known	(muy) conocido
	Welsh	galés/galesa
	west	el oeste
	western (film)	la película del oeste
	West Indian	el antillano/la antillana
	wet	mojado
	what?	¿cómo?, ¿cuál?, ¿qué?
	what are they?	¿qué son?
	what are you going to do? (*tú*, informal)	¿qué vas a hacer?
	what colour is/are ...?	¿de qué color es/son ...?
	what do you do? (*tú*, infórmal)	¿qué haces?
	what do you like doing? (*tú*, informal)	¿qué te gusta hacer?
	what is it?	¿qué es?
	what is there?	¿qué hay?
	what is the weather like?	¿qué tiempo hace?
	what languages do you speak? (*tú*, informal)	¿qué idiomas hablas?
	what's it like?	¿cómo es?
	what's the matter?	¿qué te pasa?
	what's your name? (*tú*, informal)	¿cómo te llamas?
	what time ...?	¿a qué hora ...?
	what time is it?	¿qué hora es?
	wheel	la rueda
	wheelchair	la silla de ruedas
	when?	¿cuándo?
	when is your birthday? (*tú*, informal)	¿cuándo es tu cumpleaños?
	where?	¿dónde?
	where are you from? (*tú*, informal)	¿de dónde eres?
	where are you going? (*tú*, informal)	¿adónde vas?

■ = masculine noun ■ = feminine noun ■ = verb ■ = adjective

	where does he/she live?	¿dónde vive?
	where do you live? (*tú*, informal)	¿dónde vives?
	where is it?	¿dónde está?
	where shall we meet?	¿dónde nos encontramos?
	where (to)?	¿adónde?
	which?	¿cuál?
	white	blanco
	whiteboard	la pizarra
	who?	¿quién?
	whole	entero
	why?	¿por qué?
	why not?	¿por qué no?
	wide	ancho
	width	la anchura
	wife	la mujer
	wild	salvaje
to	**win**	ganar
	wind	el viento
	window	la ventana
I go	**windsurfing**	hago windsurf(ing)
it's	**windy**	hace viento
	wine	el vino
	winner	el ganador/la ganadora
	winter	el invierno
	with	con
	with me	conmigo
	without	sin
to	**wish**	desear
best	**wishes**	saludos
	wonderful	estupendo
	wood	la madera
	wool	la lana
	word	la palabra
	work	el trabajo
to	**work**	trabajar
	world	el mundo
	worried	preocupado
to	**worry**	preocuparse
	worse	peor
that's	**worth**	vale
I	**would like**	quiero, me gustaría
to	**write**	escribir
	write to me	escríbeme

A B C D E F G H I J K L M N O P Q R S T U V W **X** **Y** **Z**

Xx

X-ray	la radiografía

Yy

year	el año
yellow	amarillo
yes	sí
yesterday	ayer
yoghurt	el yogur
you	tú (*informal*)/usted (*formal*)
(to) you	te, ti
young	joven
younger brother/sister	el hermano pequeño/la hermana pequeña
young people	los jóvenes
your (*tú*, informal)	tu/tus
yours	tuyo
youth hostel	el albergue juvenil

Zz

zebra	la cebra
zero	cero
zone	la zona
zoo	el zoo
zoologist	el zoólogo/la zoólogo

Appendix

los números		numbers
cero	0	zero
uno/a	1	one
dos	2	two
tres	3	three
cuatro	4	four
cinco	5	five
seis	6	six
siete	7	seven
ocho	8	eight
nueve	9	nine
diez	10	ten
once	11	eleven
doce	12	twelve
trece	13	thirteen
catorce	14	fourteen
quince	15	fifteen
dieciséis	16	sixteen
diecisiete	17	seventeen
dieciocho	18	eighteen
diecinueve	19	nineteen
veinte	20	twenty
veintiuno/a	21	twenty-one
veintidós	22	twenty-two
treinta	30	thirty
treinta y uno/a	31	thirty-one
treinta y dos	32	thirty-two
cuarenta	40	forty
cincuenta	50	fifty
sesenta	60	sixty
setenta	70	seventy
ochenta	80	eighty
noventa	90	ninety
cien(to)	100	one hundred
doscientos/as	200	two hundred
trescientos/as	300	three hundred
cuatrocientos/as	400	four hundred
quinientos/as	500	five hundred
mil	1000	one thousand
dos mil	2000	two thousand
un millón	1 000 000	one million

A B C D E F G H I J K L M N O P Q R S T U V W X Y Z

los números ordinales	ordinal numbers
primero/a, 1° or 1ª	first, 1st
segundo/a, 2° or 2ª	second, 2nd
tercero/a, 3° or 3ª	third, 3rd
cuarto/a	fourth
quinto/a	fifth
sexto/a	sixth
séptimo/a	seventh
octavo/a	eighth
noveno/a	ninth
décimo/a	tenth

los días de la semana	days of the week
lunes	Monday
martes	Tuesday
miércoles	Wednesday
jueves	Thursday
viernes	Friday
sábado	Saturday
domingo	Sunday

los meses	months of the year
enero	January
febrero	February
marzo	March
abril	April
mayo	May
junio	June
julio	July
agosto	August
septiembre, setiembre	September
octubre	October
noviembre	November
diciembre	December

las estaciones	seasons
la primavera	spring
el verano	summer
el otoño	autumn
el invierno	winter

= masculine noun = feminine noun = verb = adjectiv

telling the time

¿qué hora es?	what time is it?

the hours

es la una	it's one o'clock
son las dos	it's two o'clock

minutes past the hour

son las tres y cinco	it's five past three (3:05)
son las tres y diez	it's ten past three (3:10)

minutes to the hour

son las cuatro menos cinco	it's five to four (3:55)
son las cuatro menos diez	it's ten to four (3:50)

quarter and half hours

son las tres y cuarto	it's quarter past three (3:15)
son las tres y media	it's half past three (3:30)
son las cuatro menos cuarto	it's quarter to four (3:45)

midday and midnight

es el mediodía	it's 12 noon
es la medianoche	it's 12 midnight

24-hour clock

trece horas	13:00
catorce horas y cinco	13:05
son las veintiós horas y trece minutos	it's 22:13

verbs

-ar verbs
yo estudi**o**
tú estudi**as**
él/ella/usted estudi**a**
nosotros estudi**amos**
vosotros estudi**áis**
ellos/ellas/ustedes estudi**an**

-er verbs
yo com**o**
tú com**es**
él/ella/usted com**e**
nosotros com**emos**
vosotros com**éis**
ellos/ellas/ustedes com**en**

-ir verbs
yo viv**o**
tú viv**es**
él/ella/usted viv**e**
nosotros viv**imos**
vosotros viv**ís**
ellos/ellas/ustedes viv**en**

ir – to go
yo voy
tú vas
él/ella/usted va
nosotros vamos
vosotros vais
ellos/ellas/ustedes van

tener – to have
yo tengo
tú tienes
él/ella/usted tiene
nosotros tenemos
vosotros tenéis
ellos/ellas/ustedes tienen

hacer – to make/do
yo hago
tú haces
él/ella/usted hace
nosotros hacemos
vosotros hacéis
ellos/ellas/ustedes hacen

■ = masculine noun ■ = feminine noun ■ = verb ■ = adjectiv